TEACHER'S PET PUBLICATIONS

PUZZLE PACK
for
Island of the Blue Dolphins

based on the book by
Scott O'Dell

Written by
Mary B. Collins

© 2005 Teacher's Pet Publications
All Rights Reserved

The materials in this packet are copyrighted
by Teacher's Pet Publications, Inc.

These pages may be duplicated by the purchaser
for use in the purchaser's own classroom.

Copying any of these materials and distributing them
for any other purpose is a violation of the copyright laws.

© 2005 Teacher's Pet Publications, Inc.
www.tpet.com

INTRODUCTION
If you already own the LitPlan for this title, this Puzzle Pack will refresh your Unit Resource Materials and Vocabulary Resource Materials sections plus give you additional materials you can substitute into the tests. If you do not already have a complete LitPlan, these pages will give you some supplemental materials to use with your own plan. There are two main groups of materials: one set for unit words (such as characters' names, symbols, places, etc.) and one set for vocabulary words associated with the book.

WORD LIST
There is a word list for both the unit words and the vocabulary words. These lists show you which words are being used in the materials and the clues or definitions being used for those words. You may want to give students a word list with clues/definitions to help them, or you may want students to only have a word list (without clues/definitions) if you want them to work a little harder. Both are available for duplication. The word lists can also be your "calling key" for the bingo games.

FILL IN THE BLANK AND MATCHING
There are 4 each of the fill in the blank and matching worksheets for both the unit and vocabulary words. These pages can be used either as extra worksheets for students or as objective parts of a unit test. They can be done individually if students need extra help or as a whole class activity to review the material covered.

MAGIC SQUARES
The magic squares not only reinforce the material covered but also work on reasoning and math skills. Many teachers have told us that their students really enjoy doing these!

WORD SEARCH PUZZLES
The word search words go in all directions, as indicated on your answer keys. Two of the word search puzzles have the clues listed rather than the words. This makes the puzzle a little more difficult, but it reinforces the material better. Two word search puzzles have words only for students who find the clue puzzles too difficult.

CROSSWORD PUZZLES
Both unit and vocabulary word sections have 4 crossword puzzles.

BINGO CARDS
There are 32 individual bingo cards for the unit words and 32 individual bingo cards for the vocabulary words. You can use your word list as a "call list," calling the words at random and marking them off of your list as you go, or you could use the flash cards by cutting them apart and drawing the words at random from a hat (or box or whatever). To make a better review, you might ask for the definition and spelling of each word as you call it out–or you could call out the definitions and have students tell you the words they need to look for on the puzzle.

JUGGLE LETTERS
The vocabulary juggle letter game is intended to help students learn the spellings of the words. One sheet has the definitions listed on it as an extra help for students who need it or to reinforce the definitions if you choose to do so.

FLASH CARDS
We've included a set of vocabulary flash cards you can duplicate, cut, and fold for your students. Some teachers make a few sets for general use by the class; others make a set for each student. Some teachers duplicate them for each student and have the students cut & fold their own. You can cut out just the words and put them in a hat, have each student pick out one word and write the definition and a sentence for that word. Students then swap words and papers, with the next student adding a sentence of his own under the last one. You can have students swap as many times as you like. Each time the student will read the sentences written prior to his own and then add a sentence. You can cut out the words and definitions separately and play "I Have; Who Has?" Each student in the room draws a word and definition. The first student says, "I have (the name of the word). Who has the definition?" The student with the definition reads it then says, "I have (the name of the vocabulary word she has). Who has the definition?" The round continues until all words and definitions have been given.

Island Of The Blue Dolphins Word List

No.	Word	Clue/Definition
1.	ALEUT	Wore bone ornaments through nose
2.	ARU	Son of Rontu: Rontu-___
3.	BARBARA	California mission: Santa ___
4.	BASKETS	Tar-bottomed cookers
5.	BLACK	Sea cave with row of statues: ___ Cave
6.	BULLS	Male sea elephants
7.	BUSH	Has wound healing power: coral ___
8.	CANOE	Mode of transportation
9.	CATALINA	Island to the east: Santa ___
10.	CHEST	Full of beads and earrings
11.	CHOWIG	Karana's father: Chief ___
12.	CLAY	Unmarried signal: blue ___ mark
13.	CORAL	Island harbor: ___ Cove
14.	CORMORANT	Karana's pride sent to Rome: ___ skirt
15.	COWS	Female sea elephants
16.	DEVILFISH	Arms have rows of suckers
17.	DOGS	Wild ___ killed Ramo
18.	DOLPHIN	Good omen
19.	DRESS	Made by white men for Karana to wear to mission: blue ___
20.	EARTHQUAKE	It destroyed canoes
21.	FIRE	It reduced huts to ashes
22.	FISH	Sai-Sai: dried __ burned for light
23.	FOXES	Clever thieves: red ___
24.	GHALAS	Village on island: ___-At
25.	GONZALES	Mission friend of lost woman: Father ___
26.	INDIANS	They settled the island 2000 BC
27.	ISLANDS	Eight of them are off the coast of California: Channel ___
28.	KARANA	Survived 18 years alone
29.	KIMKI	Paddled off for far country
30.	LURAI	Female tamed bird
31.	MAGAT	Red star in the west
32.	MAH	Aleut word for good-bye: ___-nay
33.	MATASAIP	Would not return for Ramo
34.	MICE	Food robbers
35.	MON	Little Boy With Large Eyes: ___-a-mee
36.	MOONS	Units of time: suns and ___
37.	MUKAT	God who lived
38.	NANKO	Brought news of ship
39.	NECKLACE	Gift from Tutok: black ___
40.	NEE	Little Girl With Large Eyes: Won-a-___
41.	NICHOLS	Named for patron saint of sailors: La Isle De San ___
42.	NORTH	Star that does not move: ___ Star
43.	ODELL	Author
44.	ORLOV	Yellow-bearded Russian: Captain ___
45.	OTTER	Aleuts slaughtered ____s
46.	PELICAN	Used to sweep: ___ wing
47.	RAMO	Missed the ship
48.	RIBS	Whale ___ made up Karana's fence
49.	ROCK	Where cormorants roost: tall ____
50.	RONTU	Fox Eyes
51.	SAY	Island word for good-bye: pa-___-no

Island Of The Blue Dolphins Word List Continued

No.	Word	Clue/Definition
52.	SCALLOPS	Pelican dropped ___ from the sky, scaring Rontu
53.	SINGED	Sign of mourning: ___ hair
54.	SKIRT	Ruined swimming to Ramo: yuca ___
55.	TAI	Island word for pretty: win-___
56.	TAINOR	Tamed male bird
57.	TANYOSITLOP	Ramo's new position: Chief ___
58.	TIDAL	These giant waves crashed together: ___ waves
59.	TOOTH	Needed for spear: sea elephant ___
60.	TUMAIYOUIT	God who died
61.	TUTOK	Aleutian girlfriend
62.	ULAPE	Wished to marry Nanko
63.	URCHINS	Karana used their purple color for dying: sea ___
64.	WINTSCHA	Aleut word for pretty
65.	WON	Girl With Long Balck Hair: ___-a-pa-lei
66.	XUCHAL	Ground seashells and tobacco
67.	ZUMA	Medicine man killed by Aleuts

Copyrighted

Island Of The Blue Dolphins Fill In The Blanks 1

_____ 1. Wished to marry Nanko

_____ 2. It destroyed canoes

_____ 3. Named for patron saint of sailors: La Isle De San ___

_____ 4. Ground seashells and tobacco

_____ 5. God who lived

_____ 6. Paddled off for far country

_____ 7. Aleuts slaughtered ____s

_____ 8. Island to the east: Santa ___

_____ 9. Fox Eyes

_____ 10. Survived 18 years alone

_____ 11. Ruined swimming to Ramo: yuca ___

_____ 12. Aleutian girlfriend

_____ 13. Little Girl With Large Eyes: Won-a-___

_____ 14. Arms have rows of suckers

_____ 15. Little Boy With Large Eyes: ___-a-mee

_____ 16. Sign of mourning: ___ hair

_____ 17. It reduced huts to ashes

_____ 18. Aleut word for good-bye: ___-nay

_____ 19. Village on island: ___-At

_____ 20. Island harbor: ___ Cove

Island Of The Blue Dolphins Fill In The Blanks 1 Answer Key

ULAPE	1. Wished to marry Nanko
EARTHQUAKE	2. It destroyed canoes
NICHOLS	3. Named for patron saint of sailors: La Isle De San ___
XUCHAL	4. Ground seashells and tobacco
MUKAT	5. God who lived
KIMKI	6. Paddled off for far country
OTTER	7. Aleuts slaughtered ___s
CATALINA	8. Island to the east: Santa ___
RONTU	9. Fox Eyes
KARANA	10. Survived 18 years alone
SKIRT	11. Ruined swimming to Ramo: yuca ___
TUTOK	12. Aleutian girlfriend
NEE	13. Little Girl With Large Eyes: Won-a-___
DEVILFISH	14. Arms have rows of suckers
MON	15. Little Boy With Large Eyes: ___-a-mee
SINGED	16. Sign of mourning: ___ hair
FIRE	17. It reduced huts to ashes
MAH	18. Aleut word for good-bye: ___-nay
GHALAS	19. Village on island: ___-At
CORAL	20. Island harbor: ___ Cove

Island Of The Blue Dolphins Fill In The Blanks 2

_____ 1. Tamed male bird

_____ 2. Where cormorants roost: tall ____

_____ 3. Sea cave with row of statues: ____ Cave

_____ 4. Island harbor: ____ Cove

_____ 5. Pelican dropped ____ from the sky, scaring Rontu

_____ 6. Male sea elephants

_____ 7. Son of Rontu: Rontu-____

_____ 8. Good omen

_____ 9. Eight of them are off the coast of California: Channel ____

_____ 10. Made by white men for Karana to wear to mission: blue ____

_____ 11. Food robbers

_____ 12. Village on island: ____-At

_____ 13. Author

_____ 14. Mode of transportation

_____ 15. Brought news of ship

_____ 16. Karana's pride sent to Rome: ____ skirt

_____ 17. It destroyed canoes

_____ 18. Red star in the west

_____ 19. Used to sweep: ____ wing

_____ 20. Aleut word for good-bye: ____-nay

Island Of The Blue Dolphins Fill In The Blanks 2 Answer Key

TAINOR	1. Tamed male bird
ROCK	2. Where cormorants roost: tall ___
BLACK	3. Sea cave with row of statues: ___ Cave
CORAL	4. Island harbor: ___ Cove
SCALLOPS	5. Pelican dropped ___ from the sky, scaring Rontu
BULLS	6. Male sea elephants
ARU	7. Son of Rontu: Rontu-___
DOLPHIN	8. Good omen
ISLANDS	9. Eight of them are off the coast of California: Channel ___
DRESS	10. Made by white men for Karana to wear to mission: blue ___
MICE	11. Food robbers
GHALAS	12. Village on island: ___-At
ODELL	13. Author
CANOE	14. Mode of transportation
NANKO	15. Brought news of ship
CORMORANT	16. Karana's pride sent to Rome: ___ skirt
EARTHQUAKE	17. It destroyed canoes
MAGAT	18. Red star in the west
PELICAN	19. Used to sweep: ___ wing
MAH	20. Aleut word for good-bye: ___-nay

Island Of The Blue Dolphins Fill In The Blanks 3

_____

_____

_____

_____

_____

_____

_____

_____

_____

_____

_____

_____

_____

_____

_____

_____

_____

_____

_____

_____

1. Mission friend of lost woman: Father ___
2. Ground seashells and tobacco
3. Would not return for Ramo
4. Ruined swimming to Ramo: yuca ___
5. Wore bone ornaments through nose
6. They settled the island 2000 BC
7. California mission: Santa ___
8. Survived 18 years alone
9. Aleut word for good-bye: ___-nay
10. Star that does not move: ___ Star
11. Used to sweep: ___ wing
12. Missed the ship
13. Karana's pride sent to Rome: ___ skirt
14. Island word for good-bye: pa-___-no
15. It reduced huts to ashes
16. Little Boy With Large Eyes: ___-a-mee
17. Author
18. Has wound healing power: coral ___
19. Named for patron saint of sailors: La Isle De San ___
20. Little Girl With Large Eyes: Won-a-___

Island Of The Blue Dolphins Fill In The Blanks 3 Answer Key

GONZALES	1. Mission friend of lost woman: Father ___
XUCHAL	2. Ground seashells and tobacco
MATASAIP	3. Would not return for Ramo
SKIRT	4. Ruined swimming to Ramo: yuca ___
ALEUT	5. Wore bone ornaments through nose
INDIANS	6. They settled the island 2000 BC
BARBARA	7. California mission: Santa ___
KARANA	8. Survived 18 years alone
MAH	9. Aleut word for good-bye: ___-nay
NORTH	10. Star that does not move: ___ Star
PELICAN	11. Used to sweep: ___ wing
RAMO	12. Missed the ship
CORMORANT	13. Karana's pride sent to Rome: ___ skirt
SAY	14. Island word for good-bye: pa-___-no
FIRE	15. It reduced huts to ashes
MON	16. Little Boy With Large Eyes: ___-a-mee
ODELL	17. Author
BUSH	18. Has wound healing power: coral ___
NICHOLS	19. Named for patron saint of sailors: La Isle De San ___
NEE	20. Little Girl With Large Eyes: Won-a-___

Island Of The Blue Dolphins Fill In The Blanks 4

_____   1. Paddled off for far country
_____   2. Missed the ship
_____   3. Mission friend of lost woman: Father ___
_____   4. These giant waves crashed together: ___ waves
_____   5. Female sea elephants
_____   6. Units of time: suns and ___
_____   7. Medicine man killed by Aleuts
_____   8. Island word for pretty: win-___
_____   9. Wished to marry Nanko
_____   10. Mode of transportation
_____   11. Tamed male bird
_____   12. Son of Rontu: Rontu-___
_____   13. Survived 18 years alone
_____   14. God who died
_____   15. Karana's father: Chief ___
_____   16. Needed for spear: sea elephant ___
_____   17. Where cormorants roost: tall ___
_____   18. California mission: Santa ___
_____   19. Aleut word for good-bye: ___-nay
_____   20. Used to sweep: ___ wing

Island Of The Blue Dolphins Fill In The Blanks 4 Answer Key

KIMKI	1. Paddled off for far country
RAMO	2. Missed the ship
GONZALES	3. Mission friend of lost woman: Father ___
TIDAL	4. These giant waves crashed together: ___ waves
COWS	5. Female sea elephants
MOONS	6. Units of time: suns and ___
ZUMA	7. Medicine man killed by Aleuts
TAI	8. Island word for pretty: win-___
ULAPE	9. Wished to marry Nanko
CANOE	10. Mode of transportation
TAINOR	11. Tamed male bird
ARU	12. Son of Rontu: Rontu-___
KARANA	13. Survived 18 years alone
TUMAIYOUIT	14. God who died
CHOWIG	15. Karana's father: Chief ___
TOOTH	16. Needed for spear: sea elephant ___
ROCK	17. Where cormorants roost: tall ___
BARBARA	18. California mission: Santa ___
MAH	19. Aleut word for good-bye: ___-nay
PELICAN	20. Used to sweep: ___ wing

Island Of The Blue Dolphins Matching 1

___ 1. MATASAIP A. Yellow-bearded Russian: Captain ___
___ 2. ZUMA B. Author
___ 3. NECKLACE C. Used to sweep: ___ wing
___ 4. CHOWIG D. Aleutian girlfriend
___ 5. ORLOV E. Female sea elephants
___ 6. PELICAN F. Full of beads and earrings
___ 7. DOLPHIN G. Mode of transportation
___ 8. MAGAT H. Sea cave with row of statues: ___ Cave
___ 9. BLACK I. Whale ___ made up Karana's fence
___10. RIBS J. Karana's father: Chief ___
___11. CANOE K. Red star in the west
___12. SINGED L. Would not return for Ramo
___13. COWS M. Island harbor: ___ Cove
___14. CHEST N. Good omen
___15. EARTHQUAKE O. Gift from Tutok: black ___
___16. WON P. Ground seashells and tobacco
___17. GHALAS Q. Medicine man killed by Aleuts
___18. CORAL R. Island to the east: Santa ___
___19. ULAPE S. Village on island: ___-At
___20. TUTOK T. Made by white men for Karana to wear to mission: blue ___
___21. ODELL U. Sign of mourning: ___ hair
___22. CATALINA V. Wished to marry Nanko
___23. ISLANDS W. Girl With Long Balck Hair: ___-a-pa-lei
___24. XUCHAL X. Eight of them are off the coast of California: Channel ___
___25. DRESS Y. It destroyed canoes

Island Of The Blue Dolphins Matching 1 Answer Key

L - 1. MATASAIP	A.	Yellow-bearded Russian: Captain ___
Q - 2. ZUMA	B.	Author
O - 3. NECKLACE	C.	Used to sweep: ___ wing
J - 4. CHOWIG	D.	Aleutian girlfriend
A - 5. ORLOV	E.	Female sea elephants
C - 6. PELICAN	F.	Full of beads and earrings
N - 7. DOLPHIN	G.	Mode of transportation
K - 8. MAGAT	H.	Sea cave with row of statues: ___ Cave
H - 9. BLACK	I.	Whale ___ made up Karana's fence
I - 10. RIBS	J.	Karana's father: Chief ___
G - 11. CANOE	K.	Red star in the west
U - 12. SINGED	L.	Would not return for Ramo
E - 13. COWS	M.	Island harbor: ___ Cove
F - 14. CHEST	N.	Good omen
Y - 15. EARTHQUAKE	O.	Gift from Tutok: black ___
W - 16. WON	P.	Ground seashells and tobacco
S - 17. GHALAS	Q.	Medicine man killed by Aleuts
M - 18. CORAL	R.	Island to the east: Santa ___
V - 19. ULAPE	S.	Village on island: ___-At
D - 20. TUTOK	T.	Made by white men for Karana to wear to mission: blue ___
B - 21. ODELL	U.	Sign of mourning: ___ hair
R - 22. CATALINA	V.	Wished to marry Nanko
X - 23. ISLANDS	W.	Girl With Long Balck Hair: ___-a-pa-lei
P - 24. XUCHAL	X.	Eight of them are off the coast of California: Channel ___
T - 25. DRESS	Y.	It destroyed canoes

Island Of The Blue Dolphins Matching 2

___ 1. TIDAL
___ 2. PELICAN
___ 3. CANOE
___ 4. TOOTH
___ 5. MOONS
___ 6. WON
___ 7. MON
___ 8. DRESS
___ 9. NICHOLS
___ 10. TANYOSITLOP
___ 11. SINGED
___ 12. CORAL
___ 13. NECKLACE
___ 14. SKIRT
___ 15. XUCHAL
___ 16. BARBARA
___ 17. ALEUT
___ 18. FIRE
___ 19. GONZALES
___ 20. FOXES
___ 21. ZUMA
___ 22. RAMO
___ 23. DEVILFISH
___ 24. SAY
___ 25. BULLS

A. Missed the ship
B. It reduced huts to ashes
C. Male sea elephants
D. Wore bone ornaments through nose
E. Island word for good-bye: pa-___-no
F. Medicine man killed by Aleuts
G. Mission friend of lost woman: Father ___
H. Sign of mourning: ___ hair
I. Girl With Long Balck Hair: ___-a-pa-lei
J. Units of time: suns and ___
K. California mission: Santa ___
L. Ramo's new position: Chief ___
M. Named for patron saint of sailors: La Isle De San ___
N. Mode of transportation
O. Needed for spear: sea elephant ___
P. Made by white men for Karana to wear to mission: blue ___
Q. Clever thieves: red ___
R. These giant waves crashed together: ___ waves
S. Little Boy With Large Eyes: ___-a-mee
T. Arms have rows of suckers
U. Ruined swimming to Ramo: yuca ___
V. Island harbor: ___ Cove
W. Ground seashells and tobacco
X. Used to sweep: ___ wing
Y. Gift from Tutok: black ___

Island Of The Blue Dolphins Matching 2 Answer Key

R -	1. TIDAL	A.	Missed the ship
X -	2. PELICAN	B.	It reduced huts to ashes
N -	3. CANOE	C.	Male sea elephants
O -	4. TOOTH	D.	Wore bone ornaments through nose
J -	5. MOONS	E.	Island word for good-bye: pa-___-no
I -	6. WON	F.	Medicine man killed by Aleuts
S -	7. MON	G.	Mission friend of lost woman: Father ___
P -	8. DRESS	H.	Sign of mourning: ___ hair
M -	9. NICHOLS	I.	Girl With Long Balck Hair: ___-a-pa-lei
L -	10. TANYOSITLOP	J.	Units of time: suns and ___
H -	11. SINGED	K.	California mission: Santa ___
V -	12. CORAL	L.	Ramo's new position: Chief ___
Y -	13. NECKLACE	M.	Named for patron saint of sailors: La Isle De San ___
U -	14. SKIRT	N.	Mode of transportation
W -	15. XUCHAL	O.	Needed for spear: sea elephant ___
K -	16. BARBARA	P.	Made by white men for Karana to wear to mission: blue ___
D -	17. ALEUT	Q.	Clever thieves: red ___
B -	18. FIRE	R.	These giant waves crashed together: ___ waves
G -	19. GONZALES	S.	Little Boy With Large Eyes: ___-a-mee
Q -	20. FOXES	T.	Arms have rows of suckers
F -	21. ZUMA	U.	Ruined swimming to Ramo: yuca ___
A -	22. RAMO	V.	Island harbor: ___ Cove
T -	23. DEVILFISH	W.	Ground seashells and tobacco
E -	24. SAY	X.	Used to sweep: ___ wing
C -	25. BULLS	Y.	Gift from Tutok: black ___

Island Of The Blue Dolphins Matching 3

___ 1. NORTH
___ 2. TANYOSITLOP
___ 3. SAY
___ 4. KARANA
___ 5. ROCK
___ 6. TUMAIYOUIT
___ 7. TUTOK
___ 8. BARBARA
___ 9. NANKO
___ 10. NEE
___ 11. ARU
___ 12. DOLPHIN
___ 13. WINTSCHA
___ 14. SINGED
___ 15. CANOE
___ 16. ULAPE
___ 17. COWS
___ 18. ZUMA
___ 19. URCHINS
___ 20. DOGS
___ 21. MAH
___ 22. INDIANS
___ 23. CLAY
___ 24. TAINOR
___ 25. OTTER

A. Medicine man killed by Aleuts
B. Good omen
C. Star that does not move: ___ Star
D. Aleut word for good-bye: ___-nay
E. Female sea elephants
F. Aleuts slaughtered ____s
G. Wished to marry Nanko
H. Tamed male bird
I. Sign of mourning: ___ hair
J. Little Girl With Large Eyes: Won-a-___
K. Karana used their purple color for dying: sea ___
L. They settled the island 2000 BC
M. California mission: Santa ___
N. Brought news of ship
O. Wild ___ killed Ramo
P. Ramo's new position: Chief ___
Q. Survived 18 years alone
R. Island word for good-bye: pa-___-no
S. Aleutian girlfriend
T. Unmarried signal: blue ___ mark
U. Mode of transportation
V. Where cormorants roost: tall ____
W. Son of Rontu: Rontu-___
X. God who died
Y. Aleut word for pretty

Island Of The Blue Dolphins Matching 3 Answer Key

C - 1. NORTH	A.	Medicine man killed by Aleuts
P - 2. TANYOSITLOP	B.	Good omen
R - 3. SAY	C.	Star that does not move: ___ Star
Q - 4. KARANA	D.	Aleut word for good-bye: ___-nay
V - 5. ROCK	E.	Female sea elephants
X - 6. TUMAIYOUIT	F.	Aleuts slaughtered ____s
S - 7. TUTOK	G.	Wished to marry Nanko
M - 8. BARBARA	H.	Tamed male bird
N - 9. NANKO	I.	Sign of mourning: ___ hair
J - 10. NEE	J.	Little Girl With Large Eyes: Won-a-___
W - 11. ARU	K.	Karana used their purple color for dying: sea ___
B - 12. DOLPHIN	L.	They settled the island 2000 BC
Y - 13. WINTSCHA	M.	California mission: Santa ___
I - 14. SINGED	N.	Brought news of ship
U - 15. CANOE	O.	Wild ___ killed Ramo
G - 16. ULAPE	P.	Ramo's new position: Chief ___
E - 17. COWS	Q.	Survived 18 years alone
A - 18. ZUMA	R.	Island word for good-bye: pa-___-no
K - 19. URCHINS	S.	Aleutian girlfriend
O - 20. DOGS	T.	Unmarried signal: blue ___ mark
D - 21. MAH	U.	Mode of transportation
L - 22. INDIANS	V.	Where cormorants roost: tall ____
T - 23. CLAY	W.	Son of Rontu: Rontu-___
H - 24. TAINOR	X.	God who died
F - 25. OTTER	Y.	Aleut word for pretty

Island Of The Blue Dolphins Matching 4

___ 1. FOXES   A. Would not return for Ramo
___ 2. KIMKI   B. Star that does not move: ___ Star
___ 3. MOONS   C. Paddled off for far country
___ 4. BARBARA   D. Arms have rows of suckers
___ 5. ULAPE   E. Units of time: suns and ___
___ 6. NEE   F. Made by white men for Karana to wear to mission: blue ___
___ 7. MATASAIP   G. Karana's pride sent to Rome: ___ skirt
___ 8. DRESS   H. It reduced huts to ashes
___ 9. ORLOV   I. Good omen
___ 10. DOLPHIN   J. Red star in the west
___ 11. BASKETS   K. Brought news of ship
___ 12. CLAY   L. Mode of transportation
___ 13. XUCHAL   M. Ground seashells and tobacco
___ 14. RIBS   N. It destroyed canoes
___ 15. CORMORANT   O. Ruined swimming to Ramo: yuca ___
___ 16. DEVILFISH   P. Whale ___ made up Karana's fence
___ 17. SKIRT   Q. Yellow-bearded Russian: Captain ___
___ 18. FISH   R. Unmarried signal: blue ___ mark
___ 19. TIDAL   S. Wished to marry Nanko
___ 20. FIRE   T. Clever thieves: red ___
___ 21. MAGAT   U. These giant waves crashed together: ___ waves
___ 22. NORTH   V. Tar-bottomed cookers
___ 23. EARTHQUAKE   W. California mission: Santa ___
___ 24. NANKO   X. Little Girl With Large Eyes: Won-a-___
___ 25. CANOE   Y. Sai-Sai: dried ___ burned for light

Island Of The Blue Dolphins Matching 4 Answer Key

T - 1. FOXES	A.	Would not return for Ramo
C - 2. KIMKI	B.	Star that does not move: ___ Star
E - 3. MOONS	C.	Paddled off for far country
W - 4. BARBARA	D.	Arms have rows of suckers
S - 5. ULAPE	E.	Units of time: suns and ___
X - 6. NEE	F.	Made by white men for Karana to wear to mission: blue ___
A - 7. MATASAIP	G.	Karana's pride sent to Rome: ___ skirt
F - 8. DRESS	H.	It reduced huts to ashes
Q - 9. ORLOV	I.	Good omen
I - 10. DOLPHIN	J.	Red star in the west
V - 11. BASKETS	K.	Brought news of ship
R - 12. CLAY	L.	Mode of transportation
M - 13. XUCHAL	M.	Ground seashells and tobacco
P - 14. RIBS	N.	It destroyed canoes
G - 15. CORMORANT	O.	Ruined swimming to Ramo: yuca ___
D - 16. DEVILFISH	P.	Whale ___ made up Karana's fence
O - 17. SKIRT	Q.	Yellow-bearded Russian: Captain ___
Y - 18. FISH	R.	Unmarried signal: blue ___ mark
U - 19. TIDAL	S.	Wished to marry Nanko
H - 20. FIRE	T.	Clever thieves: red ___
J - 21. MAGAT	U.	These giant waves crashed together: ___ waves
B - 22. NORTH	V.	Tar-bottomed cookers
N - 23. EARTHQUAKE	W.	California mission: Santa ___
K - 24. NANKO	X.	Little Girl With Large Eyes: Won-a-___
L - 25. CANOE	Y.	Sai-Sai: dried ___ burned for light

Island Of The Blue Dolphins Magic Squares 1

Match the definition with the vocabulary word. Put your answers in the magic squares below. When your answers are correct, all columns and rows will add to the same number.

A. CANOE
B. MUKAT
C. NICHOLS
D. SCALLOPS
E. DOGS
F. TUTOK
G. XUCHAL
H. NEE
I. KARANA
J. OTTER
K. PELICAN
L. RAMO
M. MICE
N. NECKLACE
O. URCHINS
P. RONTU

1. Food robbers
2. Aleutian girlfriend
3. Little Girl With Large Eyes: Won-a-___
4. Karana used their purple color for dying: sea ___
5. Missed the ship
6. Named for patron saint of sailors: La Isle De San ___
7. Mode of transportation
8. Aleuts slaughtered ____s
9. Used to sweep: ___ wing
10. Pelican dropped ___ from the sky, scaring Rontu
11. God who lived
12. Survived 18 years alone
13. Gift from Tutok: black ___
14. Wild ___ killed Ramo
15. Ground seashells and tobacco
16. Fox Eyes

A=	B=	C=	D=
E=	F=	G=	H=
I=	J=	K=	L=
M=	N=	O=	P=

Island Of The Blue Dolphins Magic Squares 1 Answer Key

Match the definition with the vocabulary word. Put your answers in the magic squares below. When your answers are correct, all columns and rows will add to the same number.

A. CANOE
B. MUKAT
C. NICHOLS
D. SCALLOPS
E. DOGS
F. TUTOK
G. XUCHAL
H. NEE
I. KARANA
J. OTTER
K. PELICAN
L. RAMO
M. MICE
N. NECKLACE
O. URCHINS
P. RONTU

1. Food robbers
2. Aleutian girlfriend
3. Little Girl With Large Eyes: Won-a-___
4. Karana used their purple color for dying: sea ___
5. Missed the ship
6. Named for patron saint of sailors: La Isle De San ___
7. Mode of transportation
8. Aleuts slaughtered ___s
9. Used to sweep: ___ wing
10. Pelican dropped ___ from the sky, scaring Rontu
11. God who lived
12. Survived 18 years alone
13. Gift from Tutok: black ___
14. Wild ___ killed Ramo
15. Ground seashells and tobacco
16. Fox Eyes

A=7	B=11	C=6	D=10
E=14	F=2	G=15	H=3
I=12	J=8	K=9	L=5
M=1	N=13	O=4	P=16

Island Of The Blue Dolphins Magic Squares 2

Match the definition with the vocabulary word. Put your answers in the magic squares below. When your answers are correct, all columns and rows will add to the same number.

A. CANOE
B. PELICAN
C. MON
D. MAGAT
E. MUKAT
F. TAI
G. MICE
H. CLAY
I. GONZALES
J. ODELL
K. SINGED
L. DRESS
M. ROCK
N. DOLPHIN
O. NECKLACE
P. EARTHQUAKE

1. Unmarried signal: blue ___ mark
2. Where cormorants roost: tall ____
3. Used to sweep: ___ wing
4. Sign of mourning: ___ hair
5. Author
6. Little Boy With Large Eyes: ___-a-mee
7. It destroyed canoes
8. God who lived
9. Gift from Tutok: black ___
10. Island word for pretty: win-___
11. Mission friend of lost woman: Father ___
12. Red star in the west
13. Mode of transportation
14. Made by white men for Karana to wear to mission: blue ___
15. Food robbers
16. Good omen

A=	B=	C=	D=
E=	F=	G=	H=
I=	J=	K=	L=
M=	N=	O=	P=

Island Of The Blue Dolphins Magic Squares 2 Answer Key

Match the definition with the vocabulary word. Put your answers in the magic squares below. When your answers are correct, all columns and rows will add to the same number.

A. CANOE
B. PELICAN
C. MON
D. MAGAT
E. MUKAT
F. TAI
G. MICE
H. CLAY
I. GONZALES
J. ODELL
K. SINGED
L. DRESS
M. ROCK
N. DOLPHIN
O. NECKLACE
P. EARTHQUAKE

1. Unmarried signal: blue ___ mark
2. Where cormorants roost: tall ____
3. Used to sweep: ___ wing
4. Sign of mourning: ___ hair
5. Author
6. Little Boy With Large Eyes: ___-a-mee
7. It destroyed canoes
8. God who lived
9. Gift from Tutok: black ___
10. Island word for pretty: win-___
11. Mission friend of lost woman: Father ___
12. Red star in the west
13. Mode of transportation
14. Made by white men for Karana to wear to mission: blue ___
15. Food robbers
16. Good omen

A=13	B=3	C=6	D=12
E=8	F=10	G=15	H=1
I=11	J=5	K=4	L=14
M=2	N=16	O=9	P=7

Island Of The Blue Dolphins Magic Squares 3

Match the definition with the vocabulary word. Put your answers in the magic squares below. When your answers are correct, all columns and rows will add to the same number.

A. PELICAN
B. SINGED
C. TUMAIYOUIT
D. GONZALES
E. ULAPE
F. TIDAL
G. CHEST
H. GHALAS
I. TAI
J. MICE
K. BLACK
L. NECKLACE
M. INDIANS
N. TOOTH
O. FIRE
P. KIMKI

1. Village on island: ___-At
2. Used to sweep: ___ wing
3. Sign of mourning: ___ hair
4. Full of beads and earrings
5. Food robbers
6. It reduced huts to ashes
7. Paddled off for far country
8. Island word for pretty: win-___
9. Sea cave with row of statues: ___ Cave
10. Needed for spear: sea elephant ___
11. They settled the island 2000 BC
12. Gift from Tutok: black ___
13. Wished to marry Nanko
14. Mission friend of lost woman: Father ___
15. God who died
16. These giant waves crashed together: ___ waves

A=	B=	C=	D=
E=	F=	G=	H=
I=	J=	K=	L=
M=	N=	O=	P=

Island Of The Blue Dolphins Magic Squares 3 Answer Key

Match the definition with the vocabulary word. Put your answers in the magic squares below. When your answers are correct, all columns and rows will add to the same number.

A. PELICAN
B. SINGED
C. TUMAIYOUIT
D. GONZALES
E. ULAPE
F. TIDAL
G. CHEST
H. GHALAS
I. TAI
J. MICE
K. BLACK
L. NECKLACE
M. INDIANS
N. TOOTH
O. FIRE
P. KIMKI

1. Village on island: ___-At
2. Used to sweep: ___ wing
3. Sign of mourning: ___ hair
4. Full of beads and earrings
5. Food robbers
6. It reduced huts to ashes
7. Paddled off for far country
8. Island word for pretty: win-___
9. Sea cave with row of statues: ___ Cave
10. Needed for spear: sea elephant ___
11. They settled the island 2000 BC
12. Gift from Tutok: black ___
13. Wished to marry Nanko
14. Mission friend of lost woman: Father ___
15. God who died
16. These giant waves crashed together: ___ waves

A=2	B=3	C=15	D=14
E=13	F=16	G=4	H=1
I=8	J=5	K=9	L=12
M=11	N=10	O=6	P=7

Island Of The Blue Dolphins Magic Squares 4

Match the definition with the vocabulary word. Put your answers in the magic squares below. When your answers are correct, all columns and rows will add to the same number.

A. TUMAIYOUIT
B. MATASAIP
C. ROCK
D. CORMORANT
E. XUCHAL
F. GHALAS

G. PELICAN
H. MAH
I. DOLPHIN
J. MOONS
K. SAY
L. MUKAT

M. BASKETS
N. MAGAT
O. NECKLACE
P. CLAY

1. Would not return for Ramo
2. Used to sweep: ___ wing
3. Island word for good-bye: pa-___-no
4. Red star in the west
5. Tar-bottomed cookers
6. God who lived
7. Aleut word for good-bye: ___-nay
8. God who died
9. Unmarried signal: blue ___ mark
10. Good omen
11. Ground seashells and tobacco
12. Karana's pride sent to Rome: ___ skirt
13. Where cormorants roost: tall ___
14. Village on island: ___-At
15. Units of time: suns and ___
16. Gift from Tutok: black ___

A=	B=	C=	D=
E=	F=	G=	H=
I=	J=	K=	L=
M=	N=	O=	P=

28
Copyrighted

Island Of The Blue Dolphins Magic Squares 4 Answer Key

Match the definition with the vocabulary word. Put your answers in the magic squares below. When your answers are correct, all columns and rows will add to the same number.

A. TUMAIYOUIT
B. MATASAIP
C. ROCK
D. CORMORANT
E. XUCHAL
F. GHALAS
G. PELICAN
H. MAH
I. DOLPHIN
J. MOONS
K. SAY
L. MUKAT
M. BASKETS
N. MAGAT
O. NECKLACE
P. CLAY

1. Would not return for Ramo
2. Used to sweep: ___ wing
3. Island word for good-bye: pa-___-no
4. Red star in the west
5. Tar-bottomed cookers
6. God who lived
7. Aleut word for good-bye: ___-nay
8. God who died
9. Unmarried signal: blue ___ mark
10. Good omen
11. Ground seashells and tobacco
12. Karana's pride sent to Rome: ___ skirt
13. Where cormorants roost: tall ___
14. Village on island: ___-At
15. Units of time: suns and ___
16. Gift from Tutok: black ___

A=8	B=1	C=13	D=12
E=11	F=14	G=2	H=7
I=10	J=15	K=3	L=6
M=5	N=4	O=16	P=9

Island Of The Blue Dolphins Word Search 1

```
C A N O E X Q H S Z T J B U L H M M N
B L J D R W O N F L U B U L L S O T Z
H L Q V T D I Z A T T M R M E A N Y R
Y P A S K H K R N N O S A I D J P T Z
N E E C C M S O W R K G F C O K O E H
A H O R K B R A O A A O O E T O R Q Y
C R U Q I X K N Y M R S X X T N L G M
I Z F R G X I F Y O A W E H E N O S L
L M M A G A T D D T N T S Z R U V Z V
E U O Q T F Q X I I A D S I R B F P T
P K O M X H R U Y D N M E A N V I T F
K A N T T P O T S A C A R C C G R K Y
I T S R A Y R T L L G H D L O O E L V
M C O Q I I E S O E H S O G U R W D Y
K N D A K K I T H U A I G W P R A S G
I F M S S T Y Z C T L F S Y I S A L X
X U S A V X F C I L A H C U X G F I V
T T B U S H W G N Y S C L A Y L R P Y
```

Aleut word for good-bye: ___-nay (3)
Aleutian girlfriend (5)
Aleuts slaughtered ____s (5)
Author (5)
Brought news of ship (5)
Clever thieves: red ___ (5)
Eight of them are off the coast of California: Channel ___ (7)
Female sea elephants (4)
Female tamed bird (5)
Food robbers (4)
Fox Eyes (5)
Full of beads and earrings (5)
Girl With Long Balck Hair: ___-a-pa-lei (3)
God who died (10)
God who lived (5)
Ground seashells and tobacco (6)
Has wound healing power: coral ___ (4)
Island harbor: ___ Cove (5)
Island word for good-bye: pa-___-no (3)
Island word for pretty: win-___ (3)
It reduced huts to ashes (4)
Karana used their purple color for dying: sea ___ (7)
Karana's father: Chief ___ (6)
Little Boy With Large Eyes: ___-a-mee (3)
Little Girl With Large Eyes: Won-a-___ (3)
Made by white men for Karana to wear to mission: blue ___ (5)
Male sea elephants (5)

Medicine man killed by Aleuts (4)
Missed the ship (4)
Mode of transportation (5)
Named for patron saint of sailors: La Isle De San ___ (7)
Needed for spear: sea elephant ___ (5)
Paddled off for far country (5)
Red star in the west (5)
Ruined swimming to Ramo: yuca ___ (5)
Sai-Sai: dried __ burned for light (4)
Sea cave with row of statues: ___ Cave (5)
Sign of mourning: ___ hair (6)
Son of Rontu: Rontu-___ (3)
Star that does not move: ___ Star (5)
Survived 18 years alone (6)
Tamed male bird (6)
Tar-bottomed cookers (7)
These giant waves crashed together: ___ waves (5)
Units of time: suns and ___ (5)
Unmarried signal: blue ___ mark (4)
Used to sweep: ___ wing (7)
Village on island: ___-At (6)
Whale ___ made up Karana's fence (4)
Where cormorants roost: tall ___ (4)
Wild ___ killed Ramo (4)
Wished to marry Nanko (5)
Wore bone ornaments through nose (5)
Yellow-bearded Russian: Captain ___ (5)

Island Of The Blue Dolphins Word Search 1 Answer Key

```
C   A   N   O   E           S   Z   T           U   L       M
B               W   O   N       U   B   U   L   L   S   O
    L       T           A   T   T   M   M   E   A       N
        A   S   K   H       N   N   O   A   I   D       P   T
N   E   E   C   C       S   O   R   K   F   C   O       O   E
A   H   O   R   K   B   R   A   O   A   O   E   T       R
C   R   U       I           N   Y   M   R   X   H       L   O
I           R               I       O   A   E       R   U   V
L   M   M   A   G   A   T           T   N   S   I       F
E   U   O       T                   I   D   M   E   A       I
P   K   O           H       U       D   N   R   C       G   R
K   A   N   T   T       O   T   S   A   C   D   L   O       E
I   T   S   R   A   Y   R   T   L   G   H   S   U   R   W   D
M       O       I   E   S   O   E   H   S   O       U   R   A
K   N       A   K   K   I       H   U   A   I   G   W   R   A   S
I           M   S   S           C   T   L   F       S       L
T           B   U   S   H       I   L   A   H   C   U   X   G   I
                                N       S   C   L   A   Y
```

Aleut word for good-bye: ___-nay (3)
Aleutian girlfriend (5)
Aleuts slaughtered ____s (5)
Author (5)
Brought news of ship (5)
Clever thieves: red ___ (5)
Eight of them are off the coast of California: Channel ___ (7)
Female sea elephants (4)
Female tamed bird (5)
Food robbers (4)
Fox Eyes (5)
Full of beads and earrings (5)
Girl With Long Balck Hair: ___-a-pa-lei (3)
God who died (10)
God who lived (5)
Ground seashells and tobacco (6)
Has wound healing power: coral ___ (4)
Island harbor: ___ Cove (5)
Island word for good-bye: pa-___-no (3)
Island word for pretty: win-___ (3)
It reduced huts to ashes (4)
Karana used their purple color for dying: sea ___ (7)
Karana's father: Chief ___ (6)
Little Boy With Large Eyes: ___-a-mee (3)
Little Girl With Large Eyes: Won-a-___ (3)
Made by white men for Karana to wear to mission: blue ___ (5)
Male sea elephants (5)

Medicine man killed by Aleuts (4)
Missed the ship (4)
Mode of transportation (5)
Named for patron saint of sailors: La Isle De San ___ (7)
Needed for spear: sea elephant ___ (5)
Paddled off for far country (5)
Red star in the west (5)
Ruined swimming to Ramo: yuca ___ (5)
Sai-Sai: dried __ burned for light (4)
Sea cave with row of statues: ___ Cave (5)
Sign of mourning: ___ hair (6)
Son of Rontu: Rontu-___ (3)
Star that does not move: ___ Star (5)
Survived 18 years alone (6)
Tamed male bird (6)
Tar-bottomed cookers (7)
These giant waves crashed together: ___ waves (5)
Units of time: suns and ___ (5)
Unmarried signal: blue ___ mark (4)
Used to sweep: ___ wing (7)
Village on island: ___-At (6)
Whale ___ made up Karana's fence (4)
Where cormorants roost: tall ___ (4)
Wild ___ killed Ramo (4)
Wished to marry Nanko (5)
Wore bone ornaments through nose (5)
Yellow-bearded Russian: Captain ___ (5)

Island Of The Blue Dolphins Word Search 2

```
T A N Y O S I T L O P X U C H A L T K
M W R B D O L P H I N T L A M X B U Q
B O O T A I I T U E L M T T K X M K
U D N N B A J O M C M A G A T B N A M
L J I V S U R O S X E O V L G U N I I
L G A A S I S T W N R H O I K R T Y C
S K T Y A L C H O W I G N N C A N O E
K A R R Y A R K C K F A E A S A D U K
M Z U M A R O P M D C C G M N E O I S
T L F W V O C I Y I K Q N K L X R T B
C D O G S C K B L L K E O L C I N G
Z H X R A M O E A R E I R F B B O A O
D R E S S H P C F W T S T S O A V R N
Z H S S A U E Z I D I L H M T S S O Z
B T W M T J L Y S J D A W U T K K M A
G H A L A S M A H T A N L K E E I R L
B L A C K A R U P D L D M A R T R O E
E A R T H Q U A K E W S Y T C S T C S
```

Aleut word for good-bye: ___-nay (3)
Aleutian girlfriend (5)
Aleuts slaughtered ____s (5)
Author (5)
Brought news of ship (5)
Clever thieves: red ___ (5)
Eight of them are off the coast of California: Channel ___ (7)
Female sea elephants (4)
Female tamed bird (5)
Food robbers (4)
Full of beads and earrings (5)
Gift from Tutok: black ___ (8)
Girl With Long Balck Hair: ___-a-pa-lei (3)
God who died (10)
God who lived (5)
Good omen (7)
Ground seashells and tobacco (6)
Has wound healing power: coral ___ (4)
Island harbor: ___ Cove (5)
Island to the east: Santa ___ (8)
Island word for good-bye: pa-___-no (3)
Island word for pretty: win-___ (3)
It destroyed canoes (10)
It reduced huts to ashes (4)
Karana's father: Chief ___ (6)
Karana's pride sent to Rome: ___ skirt (9)
Little Boy With Large Eyes: ___-a-mee (3)
Little Girl With Large Eyes: Won-a-___ (3)
Made by white men for Karana to wear to mission: blue ___ (5)
Male sea elephants (5)
Medicine man killed by Aleuts (4)
Missed the ship (4)
Mission friend of lost woman: Father ___ (8)
Mode of transportation (5)
Needed for spear: sea elephant ___ (5)
Paddled off for far country (5)
Ramo's new position: Chief ___ (11)
Red star in the west (5)
Ruined swimming to Ramo: yuca ___ (5)
Sai-Sai: dried __ burned for light (4)
Sea cave with row of statues: ___ Cave (5)
Son of Rontu: Rontu-___ (3)
Star that does not move: ___ Star (5)
Tamed male bird (6)
Tar-bottomed cookers (7)
These giant waves crashed together: ___ waves (5)
Units of time: suns and ___ (5)
Unmarried signal: blue ___ mark (4)
Used to sweep: ___ wing (7)
Village on island: ___-At (6)
Whale ___ made up Karana's fence (4)
Where cormorants roost: tall ____ (4)
Wild ___ killed Ramo (4)
Wished to marry Nanko (5)
Wore bone ornaments through nose (5)
Would not return for Ramo (8)
Yellow-bearded Russian: Captain ___ (5)

Island Of The Blue Dolphins Word Search 2 Answer Key

```
T  A  N  Y  O  S  I  T  L  O  P  X  U  C  H  A  L  T
M  W  R     D  O  L  P  H  I  N        A        T     U
B  O  O  T  A  I  I  T  U  E  L  A     T        M     M
U     N  N  B  A     O        M  A  G  A  T        A  M
L     I     S  U     O  S     E  O     L     U     I  I
L     A  A  S     S  T  W     R     O  I        T  Y  C
S        T  Y  A  L  C  H  O  W  I  G  N  N  C  A  N  O  E
      A     R  Y  A  R        C  K  F  A  E  A  S  A  D  U  K
M  Z  U  M  A  R  O        M     C  C        N  E  O  I
   L  F        O  C  I     I  K     N  K  L     R  T
C  D  O  G  S  C  K     L  L     E  O  L     I  L  N  G
   H  X  R  A  M  O  E     A     I  R     B  B  O  A  O
D  R  E  S  S  H  P  C  F     T  S  T  S  O  A  V  R  N
   S  S  A  U     E  I     I  L  H  M  T  S  S  O  Z
         M  T        L     S  D  A     U  T  K  K  M  A
G  H  A  L  A  S     A     H  A  N     K  E  E  I  R  L
B  L  A  C  K  A  R  U  P     L  D     A  R  T  R  O  E
E  A  R  T  H  Q  U  A  K  E     S     T     S  T  C  S
```

Aleut word for good-bye: ___-nay (3)
Aleutian girlfriend (5)
Aleuts slaughtered ____s (5)
Author (5)
Brought news of ship (5)
Clever thieves: red ___ (5)
Eight of them are off the coast of California: Channel ___ (7)
Female sea elephants (4)
Female tamed bird (5)
Food robbers (4)
Full of beads and earrings (5)
Gift from Tutok: black ___ (8)
Girl With Long Balck Hair: ___-a-pa-lei (3)
God who died (10)
God who lived (5)
Good omen (7)
Ground seashells and tobacco (6)
Has wound healing power: coral ___ (4)
Island harbor: ___ Cove (5)
Island to the east: Santa ___ (8)
Island word for good-bye: pa-___-no (3)
Island word for pretty: win-___ (3)
It destroyed canoes (10)
It reduced huts to ashes (4)
Karana's father: Chief ___ (6)
Karana's pride sent to Rome: ___ skirt (9)
Little Boy With Large Eyes: ___-a-mee (3)
Little Girl With Large Eyes: Won-a-___ (3)
Made by white men for Karana to wear to mission: blue ___ (5)
Male sea elephants (5)
Medicine man killed by Aleuts (4)
Missed the ship (4)
Mission friend of lost woman: Father ___ (8)
Mode of transportation (5)
Needed for spear: sea elephant ___ (5)
Paddled off for far country (5)
Ramo's new position: Chief ___ (11)
Red star in the west (5)
Ruined swimming to Ramo: yuca ___ (5)
Sai-Sai: dried __ burned for light (4)
Sea cave with row of statues: ___ Cave (5)
Son of Rontu: Rontu-___ (3)
Star that does not move: ___ Star (5)
Tamed male bird (6)
Tar-bottomed cookers (7)
These giant waves crashed together: ___ waves (5)
Units of time: suns and ___ (5)
Unmarried signal: blue ___ mark (4)
Used to sweep: ___ wing (7)
Village on island: ___-At (6)
Whale ___ made up Karana's fence (4)
Where cormorants roost: tall ___ (4)
Wild ___ killed Ramo (4)
Wished to marry Nanko (5)
Wore bone ornaments through nose (5)
Would not return for Ramo (8)
Yellow-bearded Russian: Captain ___ (5)

Island Of The Blue Dolphins Word Search 3

```
T S P B S G O N Z A L E S T T R I K S
U T I E U B K E B U L L D U F I R E
T E K N L S J C O D R R K I M K I A W
O K Q B I H K M T Z O S F A K A C S I
K S H M J E C L Y A T D C I I N E D N
G A W L T I D A L I B E F K Y N C E T
J B D A N O N C N C P L R O O I T V S
K B K T L A Z E X A W L S R U H O I C
C U L P R L S J L Y T I T M I O O L H
M J H A V D N U G A T H A A T L H F A
F I K R C O O L G L R X I T S I I I
N S X A M K O A O C R U N A E S S S N
P P Q B E P M P J R O P S H O M H D
V O L R O U R C H I N S R A C A L I
D L A A N Z B H F L T A K I S A L A A
W L H B A F G O I M U L N P B R N R N
J A C Q C K Q W S T A L K O R N D A S
J C U Z U M A I H P H H W C O J S I Y
W S X P K J N G Z A F D G P O A L E U T
D R E S S W O C M F O X E S N D O G S
```

ALEUT	DRESS	MOONS	SCALLOPS
ARU	FIRE	MUKAT	SINGED
BARBARA	FISH	NANKO	SKIRT
BASKETS	FOXES	NECKLACE	TAI
BLACK	GHALAS	NEE	TAINOR
BULLS	GONZALES	NICHOLS	TANYOSITLOP
BUSH	INDIANS	NORTH	TIDAL
CANOE	ISLANDS	ODELL	TOOTH
CHEST	KARANA	ORLOV	TUMAIYOUIT
CHOWIG	KIMKI	OTTER	TUTOK
CLAY	LURAI	PELICAN	ULAPE
CORAL	MAGAT	RAMO	URCHINS
COWS	MAH	RIBS	WINTSCHA
DEVILFISH	MATASAIP	ROCK	WON
DOGS	MICE	RONTU	XUCHAL
DOLPHIN	MON	SAY	ZUMA

Island Of The Blue Dolphins Word Search 3 Answer Key

```
T   S   P   B       G   O   N   Z   A   L   E   S       T   R   I   K   S
U   T   I   E   U           E   B   U   L   L   S       U   F   I   R   E
T   E       N   L   S       C   O   R   K   I   M   K   I   T       W
O   K       N   G   I   H   K       T       O   S   A   I   A       I
K   S           E   C   L       A   T   D   C   A   K   N   C   D   N
    A           T   I   D   A   L   I   P   E   R       N   E   E   T
    B       A       O   N   C       N       L   S   O   N   T   V   S
    B   K   L   P   A   S       L   Y   T   L   T   R   I   O   I   C
    U   L   A   R       N   U       G   A   L   H   M   C   O   L   H
M   I   H   R   C   O   O       G   L   R   I   A       H   T   F   A
N   S   K   A   M   K   O   A   O   C   R   N   S   C   O   H   I   I
    P   B   B   E       M   P       I   O   O   A   I   L   I   S   N
V   O   L   R   O   U   R   C   H   I   N   S   R   B   S   M   H   D
    L   A   A   N   B       H   O   T   U   A   P   O   S   A   L   I
    L   H   B       C       F   I   A   U   N   K   O   S   R   U   A
    A   C       Z   U   M   A   S   L       P   O   S   S   D   R   N
    C   U       U           I   H       H   K   C   A   L       A   S
    S   X           G       G   H   A   W   H   O       L   E   I   T
D   R   E   S   S   W   O   C   M   F   O   X   E   S   N   D   O   G   S
```

ALEUT	DRESS	MOONS	SCALLOPS
ARU	FIRE	MUKAT	SINGED
BARBARA	FISH	NANKO	SKIRT
BASKETS	FOXES	NECKLACE	TAI
BLACK	GHALAS	NEE	TAINOR
BULLS	GONZALES	NICHOLS	TANYOSITLOP
BUSH	INDIANS	NORTH	TIDAL
CANOE	ISLANDS	ODELL	TOOTH
CHEST	KARANA	ORLOV	TUMAIYOUIT
CHOWIG	KIMKI	OTTER	TUTOK
CLAY	LURAI	PELICAN	ULAPE
CORAL	MAGAT	RAMO	URCHINS
COWS	MAH	RIBS	WINTSCHA
DEVILFISH	MATASAIP	ROCK	WON
DOGS	MICE	RONTU	XUCHAL
DOLPHIN	MON	SAY	ZUMA

Island Of The Blue Dolphins Word Search 4

```
S B I R Z I N D I A N S A L A H G T X
G K Z J U T P D H P O H M O O N S N U
O T I K M R U C T U A I Y O N U T N C
D D G R A T S T P M C A N N C F N A H
T K V T T V C O R O R A N T I A N A L
R D E G N I S J C K Y F M N C R S K P
W L M I J D K C A L B T I A A O H K N
L R W T N O R T H O T T E R G C W O T
U D H A I Q F E V O Z M A A E A L S N
R M L K H X C O F I W B A K C T A K Y
A S Z U P A L R K T R I E H I O A K F
I V I M L R A M O A P K G S E D I L O
N A D K O U I O B C A W O C E E N T X
T X C N D K T K P U K Y I V U L O B E
C E T T W H M W Q S N M I R N L R J S
N U B G B E T H C A G L C A N O E F S
G L V T E U T N T Y F H O H D R E S H
L A Y N E R L K B I I Q R K E B U S P
Y P C L A S C L S N D M A T A S I B Y
R E A E P K C H S B M J L A D I T B Y
```

ALEUT	DRESS	MOONS	SKIRT
ARU	EARTHQUAKE	MUKAT	TAI
BARBARA	FIRE	NANKO	TAINOR
BLACK	FISH	NECKLACE	TANYOSITLOP
BULLS	FOXES	NEE	TIDAL
BUSH	GHALAS	NORTH	TOOTH
CANOE	INDIANS	ODELL	TUMAIYOUIT
CHEST	ISLANDS	ORLOV	TUTOK
CHOWIG	KARANA	OTTER	ULAPE
CLAY	KIMKI	PELICAN	URCHINS
CORAL	LURAI	RAMO	WINTSCHA
CORMORANT	MAGAT	RIBS	WON
COWS	MAH	ROCK	XUCHAL
DEVILFISH	MATASAIP	RONTU	ZUMA
DOGS	MICE	SAY	
DOLPHIN	MON	SINGED	

Island Of The Blue Dolphins Word Search 4 Answer Key

```
S B I R Z I N D I A N S A L A H G     X
G K   U T   H   O   M O O N S         U
O   I   M   U C T U M A I Y O U   T   C
D     R A     S T P E L I C A N   F N H
      T T       C O R M O R A N T I A A
  D E   G N I S     K   F M N C   S N L
        I   D K C A L B   I A A O H K P
  L   W T N O R T H O T T E R G C W O N
  U     A I     E V O   M A A E   L S A
  R     L K H   C O   I W B A K   T T  Y
  A S   U P A L R K T R I E H I   O A  F
  I   I M L R A M O A   K G S E   D I  O
    A   K O U I O B C   A O C E   N O  X
  T   C N D K T     U K Y I V U   O R  E
      E T     H     Q S N M I R   L R  S
  N   U       B E T H   A   L C A N O E
        L     E U     T Y F H O H D R E S S
        A     N E R L     I     R   E B U S H
        P         L A     L S N   M A T A S A I P
        E       A E       H S       L A D I T
```

ALEUT	DRESS	MOONS	SKIRT
ARU	EARTHQUAKE	MUKAT	TAI
BARBARA	FIRE	NANKO	TAINOR
BLACK	FISH	NECKLACE	TANYOSITLOP
BULLS	FOXES	NEE	TIDAL
BUSH	GHALAS	NORTH	TOOTH
CANOE	INDIANS	ODELL	TUMAIYOUIT
CHEST	ISLANDS	ORLOV	TUTOK
CHOWIG	KARANA	OTTER	ULAPE
CLAY	KIMKI	PELICAN	URCHINS
CORAL	LURAI	RAMO	WINTSCHA
CORMORANT	MAGAT	RIBS	WON
COWS	MAH	ROCK	XUCHAL
DEVILFISH	MATASAIP	RONTU	ZUMA
DOGS	MICE	SAY	
DOLPHIN	MON	SINGED	

Island Of The Blue Dolphins Crossword 1

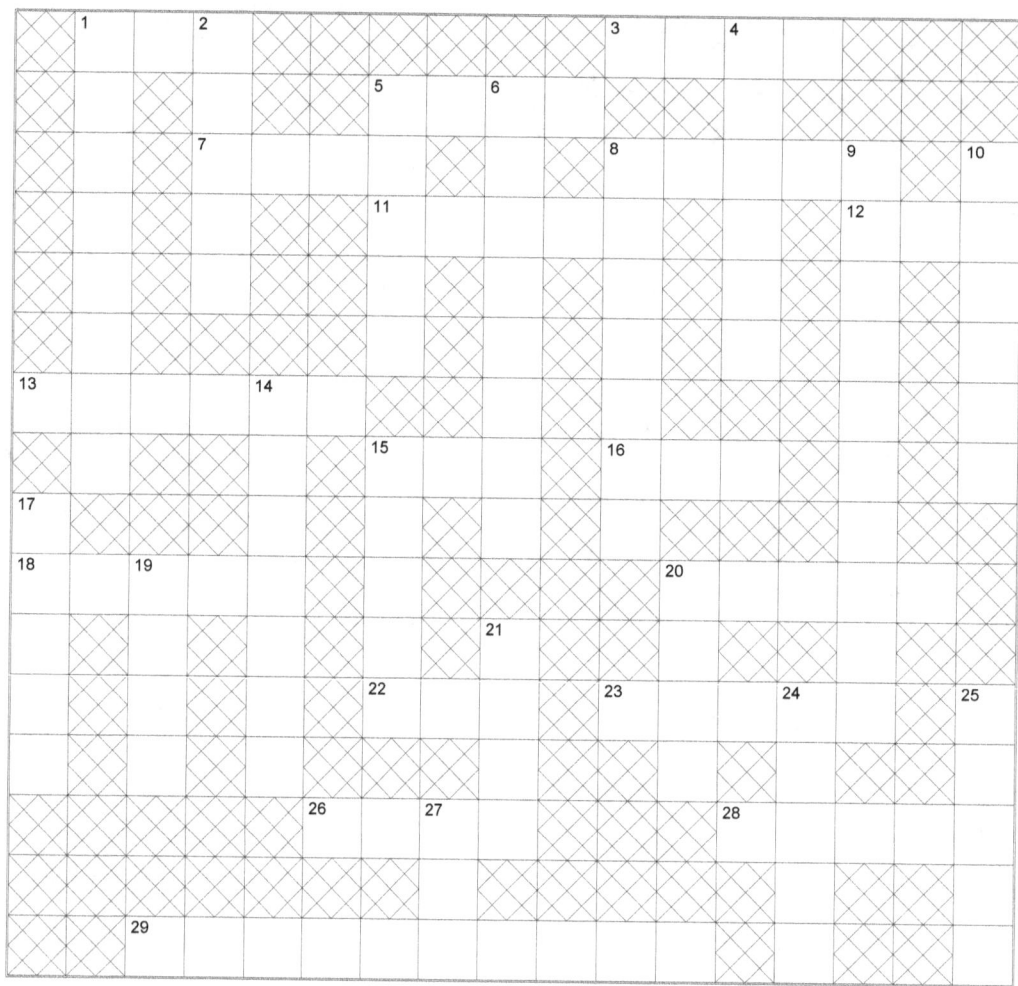

Across
1. Girl With Long Balck Hair: ___-a-pa-lei
3. Wild ___ killed Ramo
5. Food robbers
7. Missed the ship
8. Wished to marry Nanko
11. Aleuts slaughtered ____s
12. Son of Rontu: Rontu-___
13. Karana's father: Chief ___
15. Little Boy With Large Eyes: ___-a-mee
16. Little Girl With Large Eyes: Won-a-___
18. Female tamed bird
20. Island harbor: ___ Cove
22. Island word for pretty: win-___
23. Mode of transportation
26. Has wound healing power: coral ___
28. Sea cave with row of statues: ___ Cave
29. God who died

Down
1. Aleut word for pretty
2. Star that does not move: ___ Star
4. Village on island: ___-At
5. Units of time: suns and ___
6. Island to the east: Santa ___
8. Karana used their purple color for dying: sea ___
9. It destroyed canoes
10. Ground seashells and tobacco
14. They settled the island 2000 BC
15. Red star in the west
17. Wore bone ornaments through nose
19. Where cormorants roost: tall ____
20. Unmarried signal: blue ___ mark
21. Sai-Sai: dried __ burned for light
24. Yellow-bearded Russian: Captain ___
25. God who lived
27. Island word for good-bye: pa-___-no

Island Of The Blue Dolphins Crossword 1 Answer Key

	1 W	2 O	N				3 D	4 O	G	S	
	I	O		5 M	6 C	E		H			
	N	7 R	A	M	O		8 U	L	A	9 P	10 X
	T	T		11 O	T	T	E	R		12 A	R	U
	S	H		N	A		C	L	A	R	C
	C			S	L		H		S	T	H
13 C	H	O	W	14 I	G		I		16 N	H	A
	A		N	15 M	O	N	N	E	E		Q	L
17 A			D	A	A		S			U	
18 L	U	19 R	A	I	G			20 C	O	R	A	L
E		O		A	21 F		L		K	
U		C		22 T	A	I	23 C	A	24 N	O	E	25 M
T		K		S		S		Y		R		U
			26 B	27 U	S	H		28 B	L	A	C	K
				A					O		A
		29 T	U	M	A	I	Y	O	U	I	T	V	T

Across
1. Girl With Long Balck Hair: ___-a-pa-lei
3. Wild ___ killed Ramo
5. Food robbers
7. Missed the ship
8. Wished to marry Nanko
11. Aleuts slaughtered ____s
12. Son of Rontu: Rontu-___
13. Karana's father: Chief ___
15. Little Boy With Large Eyes: ___-a-mee
16. Little Girl With Large Eyes: Won-a-___
18. Female tamed bird
20. Island harbor: ___ Cove
22. Island word for pretty: win-___
23. Mode of transportation
26. Has wound healing power: coral ___
28. Sea cave with row of statues: ___ Cave
29. God who died

Down
1. Aleut word for pretty
2. Star that does not move: ___ Star
4. Village on island: ___-At
5. Units of time: suns and ___
6. Island to the east: Santa ___
8. Karana used their purple color for dying: sea ___
9. It destroyed canoes
10. Ground seashells and tobacco
14. They settled the island 2000 BC
15. Red star in the west
17. Wore bone ornaments through nose
19. Where cormorants roost: tall ____
20. Unmarried signal: blue ___ mark
21. Sai-Sai: dried __ burned for light
24. Yellow-bearded Russian: Captain ___
25. God who lived
27. Island word for good-bye: pa-___-no

Island Of The Blue Dolphins Crossword 2

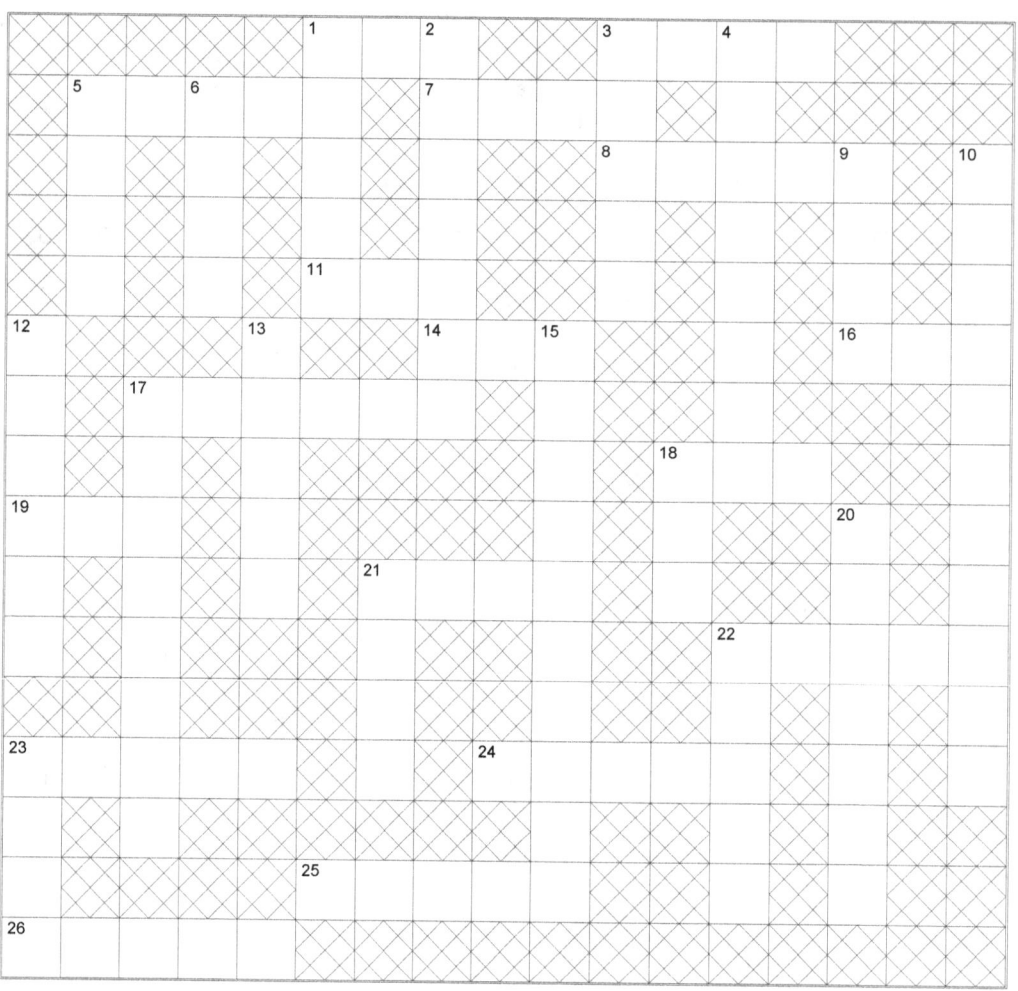

Across
1. Son of Rontu: Rontu-___
3. Food robbers
5. Island harbor: ___ Cove
7. Missed the ship
8. Aleuts slaughtered ____s
11. Island word for pretty: win-___
14. Little Girl With Large Eyes: Won-a-___
16. Island word for good-bye: pa-___-no
17. Village on island: ___-At
18. Aleut word for good-bye: ___-nay
19. Girl With Long Balck Hair: ___-a-pa-lei
21. Sai-Sai: dried __ burned for light
22. These giant waves crashed together: ___ waves
23. Full of beads and earrings
24. Brought news of ship
25. Wished to marry Nanko
26. Ruined swimming to Ramo: yuca ___

Down
1. Wore bone ornaments through nose
2. Karana used their purple color for dying: sea ___
3. Units of time: suns and ___
4. Island to the east: Santa ___
5. Unmarried signal: blue ___ mark
6. Where cormorants roost: tall ____
9. Whale ___ made up Karana's fence
10. Ramo's new position: Chief ___
12. Karana's father: Chief ___
13. Red star in the west
15. It destroyed canoes
17. Mission friend of lost woman: Father ___
18. Little Boy With Large Eyes: ___-a-mee
20. They settled the island 2000 BC
21. It reduced huts to ashes
22. Needed for spear: sea elephant ___
23. Female sea elephants

Island Of The Blue Dolphins Crossword 2 Answer Key

				1 A	R	2 U		3 M	I	4 C	E		
	5 C	O	6 R	A	L	7 R	A	M	O	A			
	L		O		E	C		8 O	T	T	E	9 R	10 T
	A		C		U	H		N		A		I	A
	Y		K	11 T	A	I		S		L		B	N
12 C		13 M			14 N	E	15 E			I		16 S A	Y
H	17 G	H	A	L	A	S	A			N			O
O	O		G				R		18 M	A	H		S
19 W	O	N	A				T		O			20 I	I
I	Z		T		21 F	I	S	H	N			N	T
G	A				I		Q				22 T	I	D	A	L
	L				R		U				O		I	O
23 C	H	E	S	T		E	24 N	A	N	K	O		A	P
O		S					K				T		N	
W				25 U	L	A	P	E			H		S	
26 S	K	I	R	T										

Across

1. Son of Rontu: Rontu-___
3. Food robbers
5. Island harbor: ___ Cove
7. Missed the ship
8. Aleuts slaughtered ____s
11. Island word for pretty: win-___
14. Little Girl With Large Eyes: Won-a-___
16. Island word for good-bye: pa-___-no
17. Village on island: ___-At
18. Aleut word for good-bye: ___-nay
19. Girl With Long Balck Hair: ___-a-pa-lei
21. Sai-Sai: dried __ burned for light
22. These giant waves crashed together: ___ waves
23. Full of beads and earrings
24. Brought news of ship
25. Wished to marry Nanko
26. Ruined swimming to Ramo: yuca ___

Down

1. Wore bone ornaments through nose
2. Karana used their purple color for dying: sea ___
3. Units of time: suns and ___
4. Island to the east: Santa ___
5. Unmarried signal: blue ___ mark
6. Where cormorants roost: tall ____
9. Whale ___ made up Karana's fence
10. Ramo's new position: Chief ___
12. Karana's father: Chief ___
13. Red star in the west
15. It destroyed canoes
17. Mission friend of lost woman: Father ___
18. Little Boy With Large Eyes: ___-a-mee
20. They settled the island 2000 BC
21. It reduced huts to ashes
22. Needed for spear: sea elephant ___
23. Female sea elephants

Island Of The Blue Dolphins Crossword 3

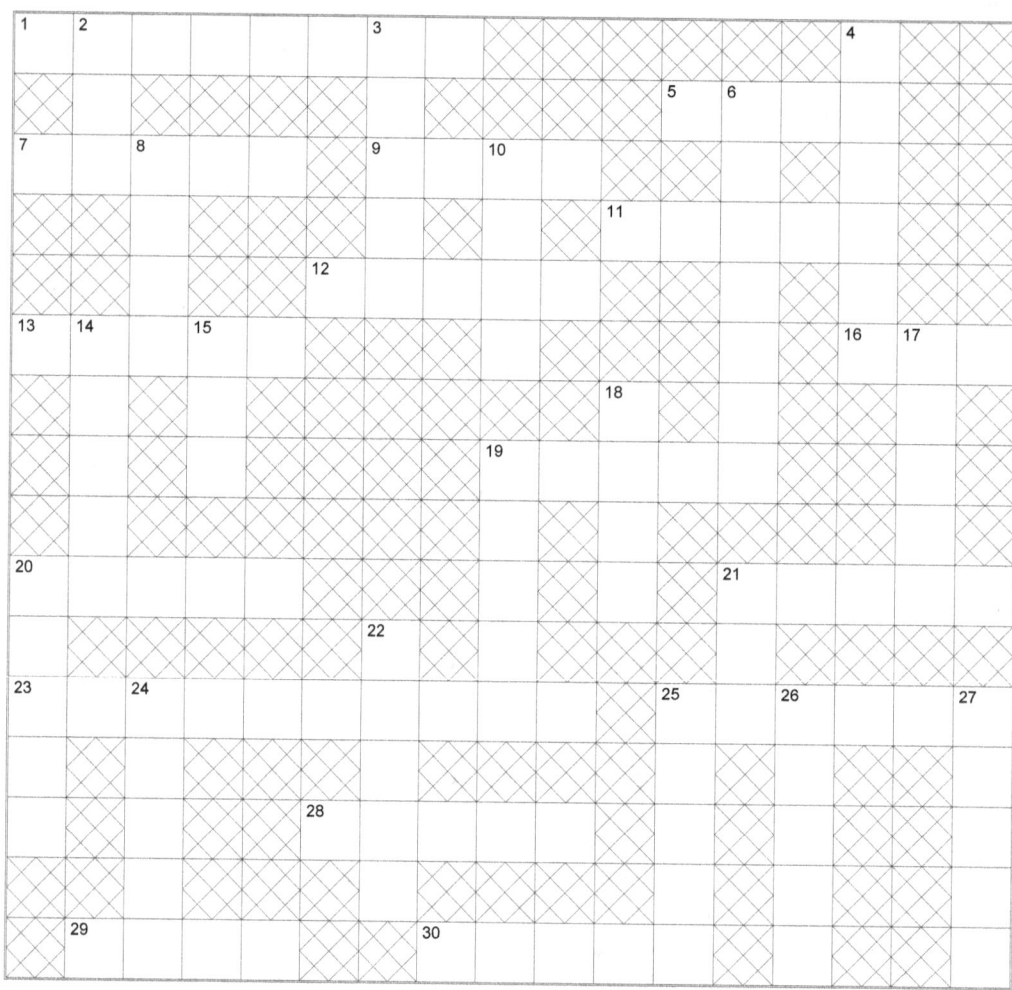

Across
1. Island to the east: Santa ___
5. Sai-Sai: dried ___ burned for light
7. Female tamed bird
9. Whale ___ made up Karana's fence
11. These giant waves crashed together: ___ waves
12. Full of beads and earrings
13. Units of time: suns and ___
16. Island word for good-bye: pa-___-no
19. Male sea elephants
20. Yellow-bearded Russian: Captain ___
21. Needed for spear: sea elephant ___
23. It destroyed canoes
25. Sign of mourning: ___ hair
28. Mode of transportation
29. Medicine man killed by Aleuts
30. Red star in the west

Down
2. Son of Rontu: Rontu-___
3. Star that does not move: ___ Star
4. Village on island: ___-At
6. They settled the island 2000 BC
8. Missed the ship
10. Has wound healing power: coral ___
14. Aleuts slaughtered ___s
15. Little Girl With Large Eyes: Won-a-___
17. Wore bone ornaments through nose
18. Unmarried signal: blue ___ mark
19. Sea cave with row of statues: ___ Cave
20. Author
21. Island word for pretty: win-___
22. God who lived
24. Fox Eyes
25. Ruined swimming to Ramo: yuca ___
26. Brought news of ship
27. Made by white men for Karana to wear to mission: blue ___

Island Of The Blue Dolphins Crossword 3 Answer Key

	1 C	2 A	T	A	L	I	3 N	A				4 G	
		R					O			5 F	6 I	S	H
7 L		8 U	R	A	I		9 R	10 I	B	S		N	A
		A					T	U		11 T	I	D	A L
		M			12 C	H	E	S	T		I		A
13 M	14 O	15 O	N	S				H			A		16 S	17 A Y
	T		E						18 C		N		L	
	T		E					19 B	U	L	L	S		E
	E							L		A				U
20 O	R	L	O	V				A		Y		21 T	O	O	T	H
D					22 M		C					A		
23 E	24 A	R	T	H	Q	U	A	K	E		25 S	I	26 N	G	E	27 D
L		O			K						K		A			R
L		N		28 C	A	N	O	E			I		N			E
		T			T						R		K			S
		29 Z	U	M	A		30 M	A	G	A	T		O			S

Across
1. Island to the east: Santa ___
5. Sai-Sai: dried ___ burned for light
7. Female tamed bird
9. Whale ___ made up Karana's fence
11. These giant waves crashed together: ___ waves
12. Full of beads and earrings
13. Units of time: suns and ___
16. Island word for good-bye: pa-___-no
19. Male sea elephants
20. Yellow-bearded Russian: Captain ___
21. Needed for spear: sea elephant ___
23. It destroyed canoes
25. Sign of mourning: ___ hair
28. Mode of transportation
29. Medicine man killed by Aleuts
30. Red star in the west

Down
2. Son of Rontu: Rontu-___
3. Star that does not move: ___ Star
4. Village on island: ___-At
6. They settled the island 2000 BC
8. Missed the ship
10. Has wound healing power: coral ___
14. Aleuts slaughtered ___s
15. Little Girl With Large Eyes: Won-a-___
17. Wore bone ornaments through nose
18. Unmarried signal: blue ___ mark
19. Sea cave with row of statues: ___ Cave
20. Author
21. Island word for pretty: win-___
22. God who lived
24. Fox Eyes
25. Ruined swimming to Ramo: yuca ___
26. Brought news of ship
27. Made by white men for Karana to wear to mission: blue ___

Island Of The Blue Dolphins Crossword 4

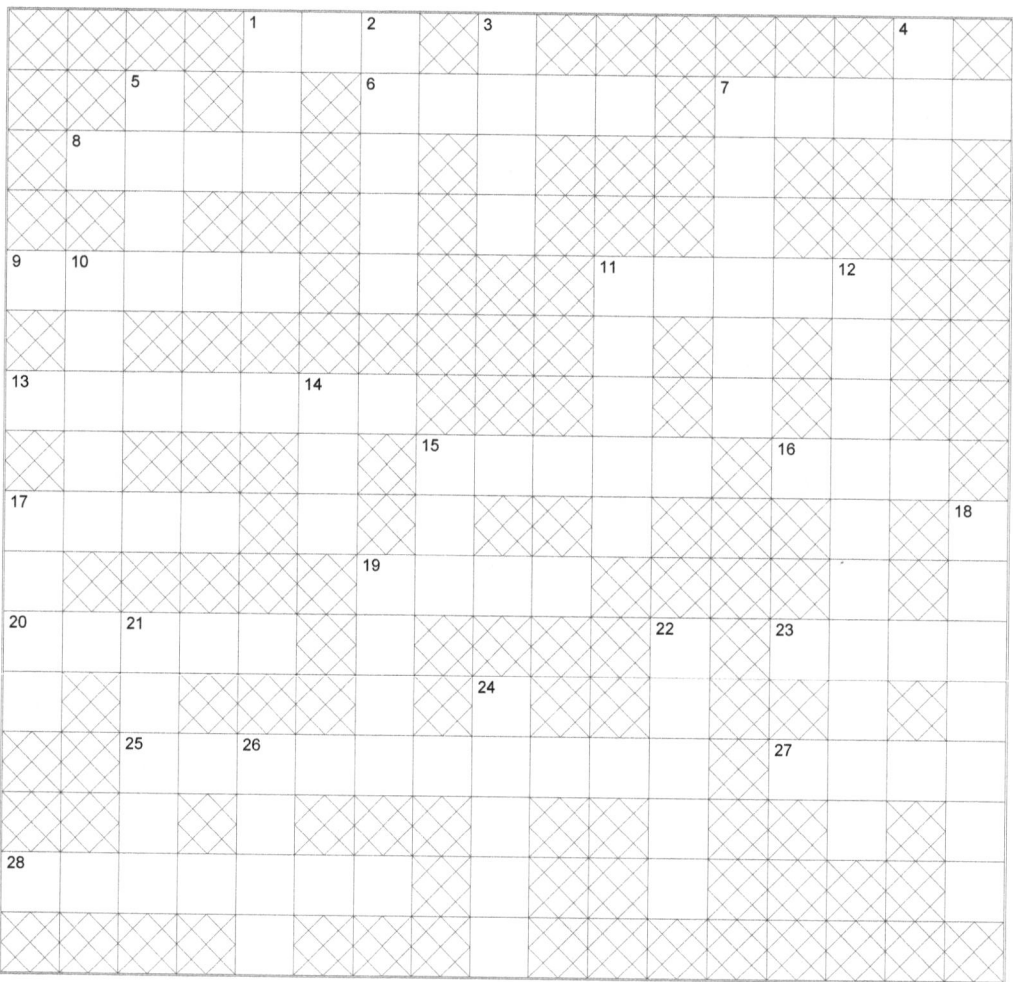

Across
1. Little Boy With Large Eyes: ___-a-mee
6. Yellow-bearded Russian: Captain ___
7. Ruined swimming to Ramo: yuca ___
8. Has wound healing power: coral ___
9. Sea cave with row of statues: ___ Cave
11. Red star in the west
13. Karana used their purple color for dying: sea ___
15. These giant waves crashed together: ___ waves
16. Island word for good-bye: pa-___-no
17. Whale ___ made up Karana's fence
19. It reduced huts to ashes
20. Units of time: suns and ___
23. Female sea elephants
25. It destroyed canoes
27. Food robbers
28. Used to sweep: ___ wing

Down
1. Aleut word for good-bye: ___-nay
2. Star that does not move: ___ Star
3. Unmarried signal: blue ___ mark
4. Son of Rontu: Rontu-___
5. Medicine man killed by Aleuts
7. Sign of mourning: ___ hair
10. Female tamed bird
11. God who lived
12. God who died
14. Little Girl With Large Eyes: Won-a-___
15. Island word for pretty: win-___
17. Missed the ship
18. Tar-bottomed cookers
19. Sai-Sai: dried __ burned for light
21. Author
22. Full of beads and earrings
24. Male sea elephants
26. Where cormorants roost: tall ____

Island Of The Blue Dolphins Crossword 4 Answer Key

			1 M	2 O	N		3 C				4 A	
		5 Z		A		6 O	R	L	O	V	7 S	K	I	R	T
	8 B	U	S	H		R		A			I		U	
		M				T		Y			N			
9 B	10 L	A	C	K		H				11 M	A	G	12 T	
	U									U		E		U
13 U	R	C	H	14 I	N	S				K		D		M
	A			E				15 T	I	D	A	L	16 S	A	Y
17 R	I	B	S		E			A			T			I		18 B
A				19 F	I	R	E						Y		A
20 M	21 O	O	N	S		I				22 C		23 C	O	W	S
O		D				S		24 B		H		U			K
	25 E	26 A	R	T	H	Q	U	A	K	E		27 M	I	C	E
		L		O				L		S		T			T
28 P	E	L	I	C	A	N		L		T					S
				K				S							

Across
1. Little Boy With Large Eyes: ___-a-mee
6. Yellow-bearded Russian: Captain ___
7. Ruined swimming to Ramo: yuca ___
8. Has wound healing power: coral ___
9. Sea cave with row of statues: ___ Cave
11. Red star in the west
13. Karana used their purple color for dying: sea ___
15. These giant waves crashed together: ___ waves
16. Island word for good-bye: pa-___-no
17. Whale ___ made up Karana's fence
19. It reduced huts to ashes
20. Units of time: suns and ___
23. Female sea elephants
25. It destroyed canoes
27. Food robbers
28. Used to sweep: ___ wing

Down
1. Aleut word for good-bye: ___-nay
2. Star that does not move: ___ Star
3. Unmarried signal: blue ___ mark
4. Son of Rontu: Rontu-___
5. Medicine man killed by Aleuts
7. Sign of mourning: ___ hair
10. Female tamed bird
11. God who lived
12. God who died
14. Little Girl With Large Eyes: Won-a-___
15. Island word for pretty: win-___
17. Missed the ship
18. Tar-bottomed cookers
19. Sai-Sai: dried __ burned for light
21. Author
22. Full of beads and earrings
24. Male sea elephants
26. Where cormorants roost: tall ____

Island Of The Blue Dolphins

TOOTH	NANKO	TIDAL	DRESS	URCHINS
SINGED	KARANA	MUKAT	COWS	ORLOV
GHALAS	DEVILFISH	FREE SPACE	CORAL	MON
RIBS	ULAPE	ROCK	NECKLACE	MICE
WINTSCHA	CANOE	EARTHQUAKE	BLACK	FISH

Island Of The Blue Dolphins

MAGAT	CATALINA	SAY	TAI	FIRE
NICHOLS	SKIRT	CORMORANT	LURAI	NORTH
NEE	ISLANDS	FREE SPACE	RONTU	CHOWIG
MOONS	ODELL	SCALLOPS	TAINOR	FOXES
BARBARA	GONZALES	ALEUT	BASKETS	MAH

Island Of The Blue Dolphins

KIMKI	TUMAIYOUIT	CORAL	DOLPHIN	FOXES
MATASAIP	MAH	NICHOLS	SCALLOPS	TAI
DRESS	EARTHQUAKE	FREE SPACE	CHOWIG	BUSH
ROCK	WON	CHEST	MAGAT	RONTU
INDIANS	CLAY	NANKO	TANYOSITLOP	SKIRT

Island Of The Blue Dolphins

SINGED	FISH	PELICAN	RIBS	NEE
TIDAL	BLACK	TAINOR	XUCHAL	ISLANDS
RAMO	TUTOK	FREE SPACE	MOONS	KARANA
NECKLACE	GONZALES	COWS	ZUMA	BULLS
ODELL	CANOE	ORLOV	LURAI	DEVILFISH

Island Of The Blue Dolphins

ZUMA	WON	TUTOK	RIBS	KARANA
TANYOSITLOP	XUCHAL	SCALLOPS	RAMO	NANKO
OTTER	LURAI	FREE SPACE	MICE	TAINOR
CLAY	BARBARA	FIRE	EARTHQUAKE	URCHINS
BULLS	FOXES	TIDAL	RONTU	CORAL

Island Of The Blue Dolphins

ARU	SINGED	SKIRT	CHEST	NORTH
GONZALES	ULAPE	MAH	COWS	PELICAN
CHOWIG	NICHOLS	FREE SPACE	MOONS	MAGAT
ORLOV	INDIANS	CANOE	MUKAT	NEE
MATASAIP	DEVILFISH	ROCK	GHALAS	BUSH

Island Of The Blue Dolphins

NANKO	RONTU	TIDAL	CHEST	BULLS
CANOE	GONZALES	FISH	MOONS	MICE
DOLPHIN	ISLANDS	FREE SPACE	CLAY	FOXES
MUKAT	COWS	NECKLACE	DRESS	SAY
MAGAT	TAI	RAMO	SKIRT	BARBARA

Island Of The Blue Dolphins

URCHINS	INDIANS	ODELL	NEE	ROCK
BLACK	RIBS	PELICAN	LURAI	CORMORANT
CORAL	BUSH	FREE SPACE	TAINOR	CATALINA
ALEUT	TUTOK	ULAPE	EARTHQUAKE	XUCHAL
CHOWIG	FIRE	TOOTH	MATASAIP	BASKETS

Island Of The Blue Dolphins

TIDAL	BULLS	OTTER	RAMO	CORAL
DEVILFISH	TUTOK	INDIANS	FIRE	CORMORANT
ORLOV	KARANA	FREE SPACE	CATALINA	KIMKI
ARU	TAINOR	LURAI	NANKO	WINTSCHA
WON	MUKAT	PELICAN	ROCK	BLACK

Island Of The Blue Dolphins

COWS	DRESS	XUCHAL	URCHINS	MAH
ZUMA	MAGAT	MON	ISLANDS	MATASAIP
SCALLOPS	CANOE	FREE SPACE	ALEUT	BASKETS
MICE	NORTH	TANYOSITLOP	NEE	FOXES
DOGS	TOOTH	RONTU	RIBS	MOONS

Island Of The Blue Dolphins

URCHINS	RONTU	COWS	MAGAT	SAY
GHALAS	SKIRT	INDIANS	ARU	DRESS
ROCK	TUMAIYOUIT	FREE SPACE	MUKAT	WINTSCHA
BARBARA	ISLANDS	ULAPE	FIRE	TAI
PELICAN	BASKETS	NANKO	ZUMA	ALEUT

Island Of The Blue Dolphins

NEE	KARANA	TAINOR	NECKLACE	BULLS
CORAL	NORTH	MOONS	LURAI	TUTOK
DOGS	FISH	FREE SPACE	BLACK	MICE
MAH	WON	CATALINA	BUSH	KIMKI
CHEST	NICHOLS	RIBS	TANYOSITLOP	DOLPHIN

Island Of The Blue Dolphins

CORAL	GONZALES	ULAPE	TOOTH	SCALLOPS
DOGS	NANKO	ODELL	WON	TAINOR
MOONS	SINGED	FREE SPACE	FIRE	CANOE
BARBARA	MICE	KARANA	MAH	SKIRT
DOLPHIN	RIBS	MUKAT	NICHOLS	DRESS

Island Of The Blue Dolphins

ROCK	FISH	ISLANDS	TUTOK	OTTER
ZUMA	NEE	PELICAN	NECKLACE	SAY
MAGAT	TIDAL	FREE SPACE	FOXES	XUCHAL
CHEST	DEVILFISH	RAMO	CLAY	BUSH
CATALINA	KIMKI	ORLOV	ALEUT	MON

Island Of The Blue Dolphins

URCHINS	BARBARA	BLACK	ULAPE	MAGAT
ALEUT	SKIRT	SAY	NANKO	KIMKI
GONZALES	ARU	FREE SPACE	TAINOR	ODELL
CHOWIG	EARTHQUAKE	NECKLACE	MON	ROCK
MATASAIP	TUMAIYOUIT	WON	TANYOSITLOP	MAH

Island Of The Blue Dolphins

RAMO	FOXES	ISLANDS	SINGED	CATALINA
CANOE	MUKAT	BUSH	TIDAL	FISH
ZUMA	DRESS	FREE SPACE	CORAL	NICHOLS
MICE	RIBS	SCALLOPS	DOGS	TOOTH
KARANA	LURAI	RONTU	NEE	PELICAN

Island Of The Blue Dolphins

ODELL	RAMO	NECKLACE	MON	SKIRT
ULAPE	MAH	INDIANS	NORTH	MICE
KARANA	TANYOSITLOP	FREE SPACE	BUSH	TAINOR
GHALAS	OTTER	CHOWIG	RIBS	GONZALES
ARU	NANKO	ISLANDS	FIRE	ALEUT

Island Of The Blue Dolphins

CLAY	DOLPHIN	FISH	MOONS	SINGED
BLACK	ZUMA	BASKETS	TUTOK	CORAL
URCHINS	DEVILFISH	FREE SPACE	CHEST	ORLOV
MUKAT	SCALLOPS	DRESS	WON	NEE
BARBARA	DOGS	LURAI	ROCK	PELICAN

Island Of The Blue Dolphins

ULAPE	NICHOLS	DEVILFISH	SKIRT	TAI
CHOWIG	PELICAN	FISH	GHALAS	ODELL
DOGS	GONZALES	FREE SPACE	NORTH	WINTSCHA
ROCK	KIMKI	CANOE	TOOTH	ARU
CLAY	TAINOR	MUKAT	MATASAIP	ZUMA

Island Of The Blue Dolphins

BLACK	COWS	MAGAT	BASKETS	TIDAL
TUMAIYOUIT	CORAL	NEE	LURAI	BUSH
ORLOV	RONTU	FREE SPACE	MICE	NANKO
FIRE	FOXES	CHEST	MOONS	KARANA
WON	ALEUT	RAMO	EARTHQUAKE	MON

Island Of The Blue Dolphins

CORMORANT	MAGAT	MAH	BLACK	XUCHAL
ZUMA	ISLANDS	ROCK	TOOTH	MON
ORLOV	MOONS	FREE SPACE	LURAI	OTTER
FISH	NEE	CORAL	RIBS	FIRE
GONZALES	NECKLACE	NICHOLS	ALEUT	CHEST

Island Of The Blue Dolphins

COWS	ULAPE	BASKETS	DOLPHIN	DOGS
SINGED	ODELL	CLAY	TANYOSITLOP	GHALAS
MICE	BARBARA	FREE SPACE	BULLS	KARANA
TAINOR	TAI	WON	URCHINS	MUKAT
DRESS	MATASAIP	EARTHQUAKE	PELICAN	RAMO

Island Of The Blue Dolphins

GHALAS	CHOWIG	NEE	TANYOSITLOP	CHEST
TOOTH	MOONS	ODELL	ALEUT	BUSH
SAY	DOGS	FREE SPACE	MON	TAINOR
ULAPE	ZUMA	FOXES	GONZALES	NICHOLS
EARTHQUAKE	CORAL	LURAI	CANOE	URCHINS

Island Of The Blue Dolphins

INDIANS	TAI	BASKETS	NORTH	XUCHAL
DRESS	NECKLACE	MAGAT	MUKAT	FIRE
DOLPHIN	WINTSCHA	FREE SPACE	FISH	ISLANDS
BLACK	DEVILFISH	TUTOK	SCALLOPS	BARBARA
CORMORANT	MICE	CLAY	WON	OTTER

Island Of The Blue Dolphins

BULLS	ROCK	CHOWIG	TOOTH	TUMAIYOUIT
OTTER	CLAY	MON	NORTH	ODELL
DRESS	SINGED	FREE SPACE	SCALLOPS	ARU
MUKAT	CANOE	COWS	XUCHAL	RONTU
PELICAN	URCHINS	CORMORANT	WINTSCHA	DOLPHIN

Island Of The Blue Dolphins

ULAPE	WON	TIDAL	FIRE	ORLOV
GHALAS	FOXES	CHEST	ALEUT	SKIRT
BASKETS	TUTOK	FREE SPACE	BLACK	MAH
EARTHQUAKE	NECKLACE	DEVILFISH	BARBARA	SAY
NEE	CORAL	MOONS	MAGAT	BUSH

Island Of The Blue Dolphins

CHEST	NANKO	BLACK	SCALLOPS	DRESS
KARANA	CORMORANT	BUSH	CANOE	XUCHAL
NORTH	ORLOV	FREE SPACE	MAGAT	COWS
NEE	MICE	TUMAIYOUIT	FISH	CORAL
DOLPHIN	MOONS	DEVILFISH	BASKETS	GONZALES

Island Of The Blue Dolphins

CLAY	FOXES	GHALAS	PELICAN	ARU
CHOWIG	FIRE	WON	TUTOK	WINTSCHA
NICHOLS	SKIRT	FREE SPACE	MAH	ROCK
SAY	RAMO	INDIANS	TANYOSITLOP	RIBS
LURAI	ULAPE	TOOTH	BULLS	KIMKI

Island Of The Blue Dolphins

ZUMA	DOGS	ORLOV	WINTSCHA	CORAL
MUKAT	ROCK	KIMKI	ODELL	NICHOLS
FISH	ARU	FREE SPACE	PELICAN	OTTER
EARTHQUAKE	BULLS	ISLANDS	BARBARA	TUTOK
TAINOR	SAY	SCALLOPS	NORTH	MOONS

Island Of The Blue Dolphins

TUMAIYOUIT	MAGAT	CORMORANT	SINGED	GHALAS
BASKETS	LURAI	KARANA	GONZALES	CHEST
RONTU	FOXES	FREE SPACE	RIBS	NANKO
TAI	TOOTH	MATASAIP	ALEUT	NEE
DOLPHIN	URCHINS	DRESS	XUCHAL	TANYOSITLOP

Island Of The Blue Dolphins

BULLS	TAINOR	DEVILFISH	TOOTH	COWS
SCALLOPS	ISLANDS	URCHINS	CLAY	GHALAS
TAI	NORTH	FREE SPACE	KARANA	ARU
BARBARA	TANYOSITLOP	PELICAN	MICE	ROCK
OTTER	TIDAL	CORAL	RIBS	NEE

Island Of The Blue Dolphins

TUTOK	INDIANS	LURAI	CHOWIG	CANOE
MATASAIP	XUCHAL	BUSH	ZUMA	MOONS
TUMAIYOUIT	DOGS	FREE SPACE	ORLOV	MON
ODELL	NICHOLS	FISH	DOLPHIN	MUKAT
WON	CATALINA	RAMO	CORMORANT	MAH

Island Of The Blue Dolphins Vocabulary Word List

No.	Word	Clue/Definition
1.	ABALONES	edible shellfish
2.	BRACKISH	salty
3.	CARCASS	dead animal body
4.	CHAFING	rubbing
5.	CIRCLET	ring-shaped ornament
6.	CLAMOR	uproar
7.	CORMORANTS	large, web-footed sea birds
8.	CREVICES	narrow openings
9.	CURATOR	person in charge of a museum
10.	DECREED	ordered
11.	DETERMINATION	conviction
12.	DUNE	rounded hill of sand formed by the wind
13.	ENTANGLED	twisted
14.	EXCAVATIONS	digs
15.	FAGGOT	bundle of sticks used for fuel
16.	FLAILING	thrashing
17.	FORBADE	outlawed
18.	FORLORN	miserable
19.	GALLEONS	large sailing vessels
20.	GIDDY	silly
21.	GNAWED	chewed
22.	GRUEL	thin, cooked cereal
23.	HEADLAND	high point of land or rock extending into sea
24.	INTRUDERS	trespassers
25.	KELP	coarse, brown seaweed
26.	LAIR	den of wild animals
27.	LEAGUES	three miles unit of measurement
28.	LOBE	round leafy projection
29.	LURE	trap
30.	MESA	steep-sided high flatland
31.	NETTLES	plants armed stinging hairs
32.	OMEN	sign; indication
33.	PARLEY	meet; hold a discussion
34.	PERISH	die
35.	PITCH	black, sticky tar or asphalt found along
36.	PONDER	think about
37.	PROW	front end; bow
38.	PURSUER	hunter; tracker
39.	RAVINE	long, deep hollow in ground made by a stream
40.	REPROACHFULLY	with disapproval
41.	RESTRAIN	hold back; control
42.	RIVAL	opponent
43.	SANDSPIT	long, narrow shoal extending from the shore
44.	SHIRKERS	loafers
45.	SINEWS	tendons
46.	SINGED	burnt;scorched
47.	STUNNED	shocked;dazed
48.	STUNTED	shortened
49.	TRINKETS	baubles; jewels
50.	VAINER	more self important
51.	VANQUISHED	defeated

Island Of The Blue Dolphins Vocabulary Word List Continued

No.	Word	Clue/Definition
52.	VICTOR	winner
53.	WARILY	cautiously
54.	WARY	cautious
55.	WRECKAGE	wreckage
56.	YUCCA	plant with stiff pointy leaves

Blue Dolphins Vocabulary Fill In The Blank 1

_____ 1. rounded hill of sand formed by the wind

_____ 2. twisted

_____ 3. coarse, brown seaweed

_____ 4. outlawed

_____ 5. bait

_____ 6. digs

_____ 7. plants armed stinging hairs

_____ 8. dead animal body

_____ 9. bundle of sticks used for fuel

_____ 10. defeated

_____ 11. large, web-footed sea birds

_____ 12. long, narrow shoal extending from the shore

_____ 13. plant with stiff pointy leaves

_____ 14. cautiously

_____ 15. winner

_____ 16. den of wild animals

_____ 17. long, deep hollow in ground made by a stream

_____ 18. conviction

_____ 19. loafers

_____ 20. black, sticky tar or asphalt found along

Blue Dolphins Vocabulary Fill In The Blank 1 Answer Key

DUNE	1. rounded hill of sand formed by the wind
ENTANGLED	2. twisted
KELP	3. coarse, brown seaweed
FORBADE	4. outlawed
LURE	5. bait
EXCAVATIONS	6. digs
NETTLES	7. plants armed stinging hairs
CARCASS	8. dead animal body
FAGGOT	9. bundle of sticks used for fuel
VANQUISHED	10. defeated
CORMORANTS	11. large, web-footed sea birds
SANDSPIT	12. long, narrow shoal extending from the shore
YUCCA	13. plant with stiff pointy leaves
WARILY	14. cautiously
VICTOR	15. winner
LAIR	16. den of wild animals
RAVINE	17. long, deep hollow in ground made by a stream
DETERMINATION	18. conviction
SHIRKERS	19. loafers
PITCH	20. black, sticky tar or asphalt found along

Blue Dolphins Vocabulary Fill In The Blank 2

_____ 1. large sailing vessels
_____ 2. person in charge of a museum
_____ 3. bundle of sticks used for fuel
_____ 4. high point of land or rock extending into sea
_____ 5. dead animal body
_____ 6. defeated
_____ 7. shocked; dazed
_____ 8. shortened
_____ 9. thin, cooked cereal
_____ 10. den of wild animals
_____ 11. die
_____ 12. loafers
_____ 13. silly
_____ 14. baubles; jewels
_____ 15. steep-sided high flatland
_____ 16. sign; indication
_____ 17. narrow openings
_____ 18. round leafy projection
_____ 19. hunter; tracker
_____ 20. winner

Blue Dolphins Vocabulary Fill In The Blank 2 Answer Key

GALLEONS	1. large sailing vessels
CURATOR	2. person in charge of a museum
FAGGOT	3. bundle of sticks used for fuel
HEADLAND	4. high point of land or rock extending into sea
CARCASS	5. dead animal body
VANQUISHED	6. defeated
STUNNED	7. shocked; dazed
STUNTED	8. shortened
GRUEL	9. thin, cooked cereal
LAIR	10. den of wild animals
PERISH	11. die
SHIRKERS	12. loafers
GIDDY	13. silly
TRINKETS	14. baubles; jewels
MESA	15. steep-sided high flatland
OMEN	16. sign; indication
CREVICES	17. narrow openings
LOBE	18. round leafy projection
PURSUER	19. hunter; tracker
VICTOR	20. winner

Blue Dolphins Vocabulary   Fill In The Blank 3

_____ 1. large sailing vessels

_____ 2. bundle of sticks used for fuel

_____ 3. twisted

_____ 4. thin, cooked cereal

_____ 5. edible shellfish

_____ 6. trespassers

_____ 7. dead animal body

_____ 8. large, web-footed sea birds

_____ 9. narrow openings

_____ 10. black, sticky tar or asphalt found along

_____ 11. sign; indication

_____ 12. baubles; jewels

_____ 13. meet; hold a discussion

_____ 14. coarse, brown seaweed

_____ 15. salty

_____ 16. miserable

_____ 17. loafers

_____ 18. outlawed

_____ 19. burnt; scorched

_____ 20. more self important

Blue Dolphins Vocabulary Fill In The Blank 3 Answer Key

GALLEONS	1. large sailing vessels
FAGGOT	2. bundle of sticks used for fuel
ENTANGLED	3. twisted
GRUEL	4. thin, cooked cereal
ABALONES	5. edible shellfish
INTRUDERS	6. trespassers
CARCASS	7. dead animal body
CORMORANTS	8. large, web-footed sea birds
CREVICES	9. narrow openings
PITCH	10. black, sticky tar or asphalt found along
OMEN	11. sign; indication
TRINKETS	12. baubles; jewels
PARLEY	13. meet; hold a discussion
KELP	14. coarse, brown seaweed
BRACKISH	15. salty
FORLORN	16. miserable
SHIRKERS	17. loafers
FORBADE	18. outlawed
SINGED	19. burnt; scorched
VAINER	20. more self important

Blue Dolphins Vocabulary Fil In The Blank 4

_____ 1. round leafy projection
_____ 2. think about
_____ 3. remnants of a shipwreck
_____ 4. large sailing vessels
_____ 5. shocked;dazed
_____ 6. long, narrow shoal extending from the shore
_____ 7. three miles unit of measurement
_____ 8. baubles; jewels
_____ 9. chewed
_____ 10. winner
_____ 11. plant with stiff pointy leaves
_____ 12. edible shellfish
_____ 13. hold back; control
_____ 14. front end; bow
_____ 15. outlawed
_____ 16. conviction
_____ 17. uproar
_____ 18. twisted
_____ 19. rounded hill of sand formed by the wind
_____ 20. narrow openings

Blue Dolphins Vocabulary Fill In The Blank 4 Answer Key

LOBE	1. round leafy projection
PONDER	2. think about
WRECKAGE	3. remnants of a shipwreck
GALLEONS	4. large sailing vessels
STUNNED	5. shocked; dazed
SANDSPIT	6. long, narrow shoal extending from the shore
LEAGUES	7. three miles unit of measurement
TRINKETS	8. baubles; jewels
GNAWED	9. chewed
VICTOR	10. winner
YUCCA	11. plant with stiff pointy leaves
ABALONES	12. edible shellfish
RESTRAIN	13. hold back; control
PROW	14. front end; bow
FORBADE	15. outlawed
DETERMINATION	16. conviction
CLAMOR	17. uproar
ENTANGLED	18. twisted
DUNE	19. rounded hill of sand formed by the wind
CREVICES	20. narrow openings

Blue Dolphins Vocabulary Matching 1

___ 1. STUNTED   A. silly
___ 2. CORMORANTS   B. three miles unit of measurement
___ 3. PARLEY   C. round leafy projection
___ 4. DUNE   D. miserable
___ 5. PROW   E. bundle of sticks used for fuel
___ 6. CARCASS   F. cautious
___ 7. LEAGUES   G. large, web-footed sea birds
___ 8. KELP   H. uproar
___ 9. WRECKAGE   I. front end; bow
___10. SINGED   J. remnants of a shipwreck
___11. FORLORN   K. conviction
___12. WARY   L. rounded hill of sand formed by the wind
___13. GNAWED   M. shortened
___14. SINEWS   N. outlawed
___15. CLAMOR   O. coarse, brown seaweed
___16. DETERMINATION   P. chewed
___17. HEADLAND   Q. burnt; scorched
___18. LOBE   R. black, sticky tar or asphalt found along
___19. FORBADE   S. meet; hold a discussion
___20. FAGGOT   T. with disapproval
___21. ENTANGLED   U. tendons
___22. PITCH   V. dead animal body
___23. CURATOR   W. twisted
___24. REPROACHFULLY   X. person in charge of a museum
___25. GIDDY   Y. high point of land or rock extending into sea

Blue Dolphins Vocabulary Matching 1 Answer Key

M - 1.	STUNTED	A. silly
G - 2.	CORMORANTS	B. three miles unit of measurement
S - 3.	PARLEY	C. round leafy projection
L - 4.	DUNE	D. miserable
I - 5.	PROW	E. bundle of sticks used for fuel
V - 6.	CARCASS	F. cautious
B - 7.	LEAGUES	G. large, web-footed sea birds
O - 8.	KELP	H. uproar
J - 9.	WRECKAGE	I. front end; bow
Q -10.	SINGED	J. remnants of a shipwreck
D -11.	FORLORN	K. conviction
F -12.	WARY	L. rounded hill of sand formed by the wind
P -13.	GNAWED	M. shortened
U -14.	SINEWS	N. outlawed
H -15.	CLAMOR	O. coarse, brown seaweed
K -16.	DETERMINATION	P. chewed
Y -17.	HEADLAND	Q. burnt; scorched
C -18.	LOBE	R. black, sticky tar or asphalt found along
N -19.	FORBADE	S. meet; hold a discussion
E -20.	FAGGOT	T. with disapproval
W -21.	ENTANGLED	U. tendons
R -22.	PITCH	V. dead animal body
X -23.	CURATOR	W. twisted
T -24.	REPROACHFULLY	X. person in charge of a museum
A -25.	GIDDY	Y. high point of land or rock extending into sea

Blue Dolphins Vocabulary Matching 2

___ 1. GALLEONS   A. round leafy projection
___ 2. PONDER   B. black, sticky tar or asphalt found along
___ 3. LOBE   C. salty
___ 4. PARLEY   D. ordered
___ 5. WARILY   E. large, web-footed sea birds
___ 6. REPROACHFULLY   F. miserable
___ 7. PITCH   G. den of wild animals
___ 8. WRECKAGE   H. thrashing
___ 9. DETERMINATION   I. baubles; jewels
___10. CHAFING   J. defeated
___11. YUCCA   K. with disapproval
___12. GIDDY   L. more self important
___13. FLAILING   M. outlawed
___14. LAIR   N. meet; hold a discussion
___15. PERISH   O. cautiously
___16. FORLORN   P. plant with stiff pointy leaves
___17. VANQUISHED   Q. plants armed stinging hairs
___18. CREVICES   R. narrow openings
___19. BRACKISH   S. rubbing
___20. CORMORANTS   T. remnants of a shipwreck
___21. VAINER   U. think about
___22. DECREED   V. large sailing vessels
___23. NETTLES   W. silly
___24. FORBADE   X. die
___25. TRINKETS   Y. conviction

Blue Dolphins Vocabulary Matching 2 Answer Key

V - 1.	GALLEONS	A. round leafy projection
U - 2.	PONDER	B. black, sticky tar or asphalt found along
A - 3.	LOBE	C. salty
N - 4.	PARLEY	D. ordered
O - 5.	WARILY	E. large, web-footed sea birds
K - 6.	REPROACHFULLY	F. miserable
B - 7.	PITCH	G. den of wild animals
T - 8.	WRECKAGE	H. thrashing
Y - 9.	DETERMINATION	I. baubles; jewels
S - 10.	CHAFING	J. defeated
P - 11.	YUCCA	K. with disapproval
W - 12.	GIDDY	L. more self important
H - 13.	FLAILING	M. outlawed
G - 14.	LAIR	N. meet; hold a discussion
X - 15.	PERISH	O. cautiously
F - 16.	FORLORN	P. plant with stiff pointy leaves
J - 17.	VANQUISHED	Q. plants armed stinging hairs
R - 18.	CREVICES	R. narrow openings
C - 19.	BRACKISH	S. rubbing
E - 20.	CORMORANTS	T. remnants of a shipwreck
L - 21.	VAINER	U. think about
D - 22.	DECREED	V. large sailing vessels
Q - 23.	NETTLES	W. silly
M - 24.	FORBADE	X. die
I - 25.	TRINKETS	Y. conviction

Blue Dolphins Vocabulary Matching 3

___ 1. GNAWED   A. cautious
___ 2. CURATOR   B. sign; indication
___ 3. REPROACHFULLY   C. thrashing
___ 4. LEAGUES   D. bundle of sticks used for fuel
___ 5. MESA   E. round leafy projection
___ 6. WARY   F. burnt; scorched
___ 7. LAIR   G. ordered
___ 8. FAGGOT   H. plant with stiff pointy leaves
___ 9. FORLORN   I. dead animal body
___10. YUCCA   J. three miles unit of measurement
___11. ABALONES   K. chewed
___12. HEADLAND   L. large, web-footed sea birds
___13. GRUEL   M. front end; bow
___14. SINGED   N. narrow openings
___15. WARILY   O. edible shellfish
___16. LOBE   P. steep-sided high flatland
___17. CORMORANTS   Q. with disapproval
___18. OMEN   R. thin, cooked cereal
___19. CARCASS   S. high point of land or rock extending into sea
___20. DECREED   T. cautiously
___21. STUNNED   U. baubles; jewels
___22. CREVICES   V. person in charge of a museum
___23. TRINKETS   W. den of wild animals
___24. PROW   X. miserable
___25. FLAILING   Y. shocked; dazed

Blue Dolphins Vocabulary Matching 3 Answer Key

K - 1. GNAWED		A. cautious
V - 2. CURATOR		B. sign; indication
Q - 3. REPROACHFULLY		C. thrashing
J - 4. LEAGUES		D. bundle of sticks used for fuel
P - 5. MESA		E. round leafy projection
A - 6. WARY		F. burnt; scorched
W - 7. LAIR		G. ordered
D - 8. FAGGOT		H. plant with stiff pointy leaves
X - 9. FORLORN		I. dead animal body
H - 10. YUCCA		J. three miles unit of measurement
O - 11. ABALONES		K. chewed
S - 12. HEADLAND		L. large, web-footed sea birds
R - 13. GRUEL		M. front end; bow
F - 14. SINGED		N. narrow openings
T - 15. WARILY		O. edible shellfish
E - 16. LOBE		P. steep-sided high flatland
L - 17. CORMORANTS		Q. with disapproval
B - 18. OMEN		R. thin, cooked cereal
I - 19. CARCASS		S. high point of land or rock extending into sea
G - 20. DECREED		T. cautiously
Y - 21. STUNNED		U. baubles; jewels
N - 22. CREVICES		V. person in charge of a museum
U - 23. TRINKETS		W. den of wild animals
M - 24. PROW		X. miserable
C - 25. FLAILING		Y. shocked; dazed

Blue Dolphins Vocabulary Matching 4

___ 1. WRECKAGE   A. rubbing
___ 2. DECREED   B. large sailing vessels
___ 3. DETERMINATION   C. long, narrow shoal extending from the shore
___ 4. TRINKETS   D. think about
___ 5. STUNNED   E. shocked; dazed
___ 6. LAIR   F. high point of land or rock extending into sea
___ 7. HEADLAND   G. baubles; jewels
___ 8. SANDSPIT   H. hold back; control
___ 9. VICTOR   I. ordered
___10. WARY   J. twisted
___11. KELP   K. den of wild animals
___12. WARILY   L. opponent
___13. GALLEONS   M. bait
___14. LURE   N. ring-shaped ornament
___15. VAINER   O. winner
___16. CIRCLET   P. cautiously
___17. PONDER   Q. defeated
___18. VANQUISHED   R. loafers
___19. ENTANGLED   S. coarse, brown seaweed
___20. SHIRKERS   T. remnants of a shipwreck
___21. GRUEL   U. conviction
___22. RESTRAIN   V. more self important
___23. CREVICES   W. thin, cooked cereal
___24. CHAFING   X. narrow openings
___25. RIVAL   Y. cautious

Blue Dolphins Vocabulary Matching 4 Answer Key

T - 1. WRECKAGE	A. rubbing
I - 2. DECREED	B. large sailing vessels
U - 3. DETERMINATION	C. long, narrow shoal extending from the shore
G - 4. TRINKETS	D. think about
E - 5. STUNNED	E. shocked; dazed
K - 6. LAIR	F. high point of land or rock extending into sea
F - 7. HEADLAND	G. baubles; jewels
C - 8. SANDSPIT	H. hold back; control
O - 9. VICTOR	I. ordered
Y - 10. WARY	J. twisted
S - 11. KELP	K. den of wild animals
P - 12. WARILY	L. opponent
B - 13. GALLEONS	M. bait
M - 14. LURE	N. ring-shaped ornament
V - 15. VAINER	O. winner
N - 16. CIRCLET	P. cautiously
D - 17. PONDER	Q. defeated
Q - 18. VANQUISHED	R. loafers
J - 19. ENTANGLED	S. coarse, brown seaweed
R - 20. SHIRKERS	T. remnants of a shipwreck
W - 21. GRUEL	U. conviction
H - 22. RESTRAIN	V. more self important
X - 23. CREVICES	W. thin, cooked cereal
A - 24. CHAFING	X. narrow openings
L - 25. RIVAL	Y. cautious

Blue Dolphins Vocabulary Magic Squares 1

Match the definition with the vocabulary word. Put your answers in the magic squares below. When your answers are correct, all columns and rows will add to the same number.

A. GNAWED
B. SINEWS
C. VAINER
D. PONDER
E. FAGGOT
F. VICTOR
G. DUNE
H. NETTLES
I. OMEN
J. RAVINE
K. CIRCLET
L. GRUEL
M. CHAFING
N. BRACKISH
O. DECREED
P. WRECKAGE

1. plants armed stinging hairs
2. chewed
3. tendons
4. rounded hill of sand formed by the wind
5. long, deep hollow in ground made by a stream
6. ordered
7. remnants of a shipwreck
8. sign; indication
9. ring-shaped ornament
10. salty
11. rubbing
12. thin, cooked cereal
13. bundle of sticks used for fuel
14. think about
15. more self important
16. winner

A=	B=	C=	D=
E=	F=	G=	H=
I=	J=	K=	L=
M=	N=	O=	P=

Blue Dolphins Vocabulary Magic Squares 1 Answer Key

Match the definition with the vocabulary word. Put your answers in the magic squares below. When your answers are correct, all columns and rows will add to the same number.

A. GNAWED
B. SINEWS
C. VAINER
D. PONDER
E. FAGGOT
F. VICTOR

G. DUNE
H. NETTLES
I. OMEN
J. RAVINE
K. CIRCLET
L. GRUEL

M. CHAFING
N. BRACKISH
O. DECREED
P. WRECKAGE

1. plants armed stinging hairs
2. chewed
3. tendons
4. rounded hill of sand formed by the wind
5. long, deep hollow in ground made by a stream
6. ordered
7. remnants of a shipwreck
8. sign; indication
9. ring-shaped ornament
10. salty
11. rubbing
12. thin, cooked cereal
13. bundle of sticks used for fuel
14. think about
15. more self important
16. winner

A=2	B=3	C=15	D=14
E=13	F=16	G=4	H=1
I=8	J=5	K=9	L=12
M=11	N=10	O=6	P=7

Blue Dolphins Vocabulary Magic Squares 2

Match the definition with the vocabulary word. Put your answers in the magic squares below. When your answers are correct, all columns and rows will add to the same number.

A. CURATOR
B. VANQUISHED
C. GIDDY
D. VAINER
E. WARY
F. ABALONES
G. LURE
H. DUNE
I. GNAWED
J. FORBADE
K. PURSUER
L. BRACKISH
M. STUNNED
N. LOBE
O. PERISH
P. WARILY

1. die
2. outlawed
3. rounded hill of sand formed by the wind
4. person in charge of a museum
5. more self important
6. cautious
7. hunter; tracker
8. round leafy projection
9. edible shellfish
10. silly
11. shocked;dazed
12. salty
13. chewed
14. cautiously
15. defeated
16. bait

A=	B=	C=	D=
E=	F=	G=	H=
I=	J=	K=	L=
M=	N=	O=	P=

Blue Dolphins Vocabulary Magic Squares 2 Answer Key

Match the definition with the vocabulary word. Put your answers in the magic squares below. When your answers are correct, all columns and rows will add to the same number.

A. CURATOR
B. VANQUISHED
C. GIDDY
D. VAINER
E. WARY
F. ABALONES
G. LURE
H. DUNE
I. GNAWED
J. FORBADE
K. PURSUER
L. BRACKISH
M. STUNNED
N. LOBE
O. PERISH
P. WARILY

1. die
2. outlawed
3. rounded hill of sand formed by the wind
4. person in charge of a museum
5. more self important
6. cautious
7. hunter; tracker
8. round leafy projection
9. edible shellfish
10. silly
11. shocked; dazed
12. salty
13. chewed
14. cautiously
15. defeated
16. bait

A=4	B=15	C=10	D=5
E=6	F=9	G=16	H=3
I=13	J=2	K=7	L=12
M=11	N=8	O=1	P=14

Blue Dolphins Vocabulary Magic Squares 3

Match the definition with the vocabulary word. Put your answers in the magic squares below. When your answers are correct, all columns and rows will add to the same number.

A. PROW
B. CARCASS
C. GALLEONS
D. RIVAL
E. DUNE
F. YUCCA
G. CREVICES
H. WRECKAGE
I. CURATOR
J. HEADLAND
K. PONDER
L. STUNNED
M. PERISH
N. FAGGOT
O. MESA
P. LEAGUES

1. large sailing vessels
2. high point of land or rock extending into sea
3. plant with stiff pointy leaves
4. steep-sided high flatland
5. three miles unit of measurement
6. rounded hill of sand formed by the wind
7. person in charge of a museum
8. opponent
9. die
10. remnants of a shipwreck
11. shocked; dazed
12. front end; bow
13. dead animal body
14. think about
15. narrow openings
16. bundle of sticks used for fuel

A=	B=	C=	D=
E=	F=	G=	H=
I=	J=	K=	L=
M=	N=	O=	P=

84
Copyrighted

Blue Dolphins Vocabulary Magic Squares 3 Answer Key

Match the definition with the vocabulary word. Put your answers in the magic squares below. When your answers are correct, all columns and rows will add to the same number.

A. PROW
B. CARCASS
C. GALLEONS
D. RIVAL
E. DUNE
F. YUCCA
G. CREVICES
H. WRECKAGE
I. CURATOR
J. HEADLAND
K. PONDER
L. STUNNED
M. PERISH
N. FAGGOT
O. MESA
P. LEAGUES

1. large sailing vessels
2. high point of land or rock extending into sea
3. plant with stiff pointy leaves
4. steep-sided high flatland
5. three miles unit of measurement
6. rounded hill of sand formed by the wind
7. person in charge of a museum
8. opponent
9. die
10. remnants of a shipwreck
11. shocked; dazed
12. front end; bow
13. dead animal body
14. think about
15. narrow openings
16. bundle of sticks used for fuel

A=12	B=13	C=1	D=8
E=6	F=3	G=15	H=10
I=7	J=2	K=14	L=11
M=9	N=16	O=4	P=5

Blue Dolphins Vocabulary Magic Squares 4

Match the definition with the vocabulary word. Put your answers in the magic squares below. When your answers are correct, all columns and rows will add to the same number.

A. PERISH
B. CIRCLET
C. LOBE
D. GIDDY
E. KELP
F. WARY
G. DECREED
H. CREVICES
I. RAVINE
J. OMEN
K. DUNE
L. SINGED
M. VICTOR
N. FORLORN
O. INTRUDERS
P. VANQUISHED

1. narrow openings
2. winner
3. ring-shaped ornament
4. rounded hill of sand formed by the wind
5. sign; indication
6. round leafy projection
7. defeated
8. coarse, brown seaweed
9. trespassers
10. cautious
11. long, deep hollow in ground made by a stream
12. silly
13. die
14. burnt; scorched
15. ordered
16. miserable

A=	B=	C=	D=
E=	F=	G=	H=
I=	J=	K=	L=
M=	N=	O=	P=

Blue Dolphins Vocabulary Magic Squares 4 Answer Key

Match the definition with the vocabulary word. Put your answers in the magic squares below. When your answers are correct, all columns and rows will add to the same number.

A. PERISH
B. CIRCLET
C. LOBE
D. GIDDY
E. KELP
F. WARY
G. DECREED
H. CREVICES
I. RAVINE
J. OMEN
K. DUNE
L. SINGED
M. VICTOR
N. FORLORN
O. INTRUDERS
P. VANQUISHED

1. narrow openings
2. winner
3. ring-shaped ornament
4. rounded hill of sand formed by the wind
5. sign; indication
6. round leafy projection
7. defeated
8. coarse, brown seaweed
9. trespassers
10. cautious
11. long, deep hollow in ground made by a stream
12. silly
13. die
14. burnt;scorched
15. ordered
16. miserable

A=13	B=3	C=6	D=12
E=8	F=10	G=15	H=1
I=11	J=5	K=4	L=14
M=2	N=16	O=9	P=7

Blue Dolphins Vocabulary Word Search 1

```
C S C C R S H I R K E R S N O E L A G
I Q T L E D P D E T E R M I N A T I O N
R Z O A S C U R A T O R P J W B G R R Z
C Q G M T H R T R I N K E T S R F E X P
L V G O R C S E C I V E R C H A S D S F
E S A R A K U M Z N N R I P G C V N Q N
T Y F I I E E S K E Z C S R R K O O N M
J E S T N A R O M R O C H C T I P P E J
G L R I S E P O B F N T T A T S V S T C
H R V R T L R R W D O Y W A F H A A T K
P A C C U Y W H O S Y R V D S I P I L L
R P N V N Y M H L W I A L S S I N G E D
W C X M T R N D W A C Y A O G T N G S Y
S R K S E A E J L X L C M R H G E R C
V T E B D W D Y E I R E R U L N I N W W
I S U C A G Z B R A D W D G D K D L G S
C P F N K M D A C E D E C R E E D O R Z
T Q G X N A W T N H R R X D B D Y B U M
O K E L P E G U Q S A N D S P I T E E V
R F O R B A D E A B A L O N E S S T L G
```

bait (4)
baubles; jewels (8)
black, sticky tar or asphalt found along (5)
bundle of sticks used for fuel (6)
burnt;scorched (6)
cautious (4)
cautiously (6)
chewed (6)
coarse, brown seaweed (4)
conviction (13)
dead animal body (7)
den of wild animals (4)
die (6)
digs (11)
edible shellfish (8)
front end; bow (4)
hold back; control (8)
hunter; tracker (7)
large sailing vessels (8)
large, web-footed sea birds (10)
loafers (8)
long, deep hollow in ground made by a stream (6)
long, narrow shoal extending from the shore (8)
meet; hold a discussion (6)

miserable (7)
more self important (6)
narrow openings (8)
opponent (5)
ordered (7)
outlawed (7)
person in charge of a museum (7)
plant with stiff pointy leaves (5)
plants armed stinging hairs (7)
remnants of a shipwreck (8)
ring-shaped ornament (7)
round leafy projection (4)
rounded hill of sand formed by the wind (4)
rubbing (7)
salty (8)
shocked;dazed (7)
shortened (7)
sign; indication (4)
silly (5)
steep-sided high flatland (4)
tendons (6)
thin, cooked cereal (5)
think about (6)
trespassers (9)
uproar (6)
winner (6)

Blue Dolphins Vocabulary Word Search 1 Answer Key

- bait (4)
- baubles; jewels (8)
- black, sticky tar or asphalt found along (5)
- bundle of sticks used for fuel (6)
- burnt;scorched (6)
- cautious (4)
- cautiously (6)
- chewed (6)
- coarse, brown seaweed (4)
- conviction (13)
- dead animal body (7)
- den of wild animals (4)
- die (6)
- digs (11)
- edible shellfish (8)
- front end; bow (4)
- hold back; control (8)
- hunter; tracker (7)
- large sailing vessels (8)
- large, web-footed sea birds (10)
- loafers (8)
- long, deep hollow in ground made by a stream (6)
- long, narrow shoal extending from the shore (8)
- meet; hold a discussion (6)
- miserable (7)
- more self important (6)
- narrow openings (8)
- opponent (5)
- ordered (7)
- outlawed (7)
- person in charge of a museum (7)
- plant with stiff pointy leaves (5)
- plants armed stinging hairs (7)
- remnants of a shipwreck (8)
- ring-shaped ornament (7)
- round leafy projection (4)
- rounded hill of sand formed by the wind (4)
- rubbing (7)
- salty (8)
- shocked;dazed (7)
- shortened (7)
- sign; indication (4)
- silly (5)
- steep-sided high flatland (4)
- tendons (6)
- thin, cooked cereal (5)
- think about (6)
- trespassers (9)
- uproar (6)
- winner (6)

Blue Dolphins Vocabulary Word Search 2

```
F O R L O R N E N T A N G L E D E T J K
A D E T E R M I N A T I O N T D I K S N
B E X C A V A T I O N S R M A P B H S W
A S W H M R T Y W D D W L B S Z K W A D
L R B L T E N L M L S N R D P M S J C N
O E G S L H L I R K L O N P S R R T R R
N K E C S E Y R O Q F A K W E E W Y A C
E R R L W A N A M W S D I D P R Q V C V
S I N G E D E W A N G L U R E N I A V X
C H F K N L Z R L L B R O N W N C S B J
P S L R I A Y S C Q T A K M E O K H H M
A G A S S N D R M N C F N J L M K N L W
R L I B T D B R I H E G A K C E R W O C
L V L D P U E R F V N Y C G L N S R B Q
E C I R D D N U A I A Q C P G E P E E B
Y T N C N Y L N F C B L U X L O I U M T
J C G O T L D A E D K Z Y T M H T S E S
H X P W Y O H P J D Q I T Y F W C R S B
G R U E L C R E V I C E S S N D H U A X
G A L L E O N S P J N C F H Q Q D P X T
```

bait (4)
black, sticky tar or asphalt found along (5)
bundle of sticks used for fuel (6)
burnt;scorched (6)
cautious (4)
cautiously (6)
chewed (6)
coarse, brown seaweed (4)
conviction (13)
dead animal body (7)
den of wild animals (4)
die (6)
digs (11)
edible shellfish (8)
front end; bow (4)
high point of land or rock extending into sea (8)
hold back; control (8)
hunter; tracker (7)
large sailing vessels (8)
loafers (8)
long, deep hollow in ground made by a stream (6)
long, narrow shoal extending from the shore (8)
meet; hold a discussion (6)

miserable (7)
more self important (6)
narrow openings (8)
opponent (5)
outlawed (7)
plant with stiff pointy leaves (5)
plants armed stinging hairs (7)
remnants of a shipwreck (8)
ring-shaped ornament (7)
round leafy projection (4)
rounded hill of sand formed by the wind (4)
rubbing (7)
salty (8)
shocked;dazed (7)
sign; indication (4)
silly (5)
steep-sided high flatland (4)
tendons (6)
thin, cooked cereal (5)
think about (6)
thrashing (8)
trespassers (9)
twisted (9)
uproar (6)
winner (6)
with disapproval (13)

Blue Dolphins Vocabulary Word Search 2 Answer Key

bait (4)
black, sticky tar or asphalt found along (5)
bundle of sticks used for fuel (6)
burnt;scorched (6)
cautious (4)
cautiously (6)
chewed (6)
coarse, brown seaweed (4)
conviction (13)
dead animal body (7)
den of wild animals (4)
die (6)
digs (11)
edible shellfish (8)
front end; bow (4)
high point of land or rock extending into sea (8)
hold back; control (8)
hunter; tracker (7)
large sailing vessels (8)
loafers (8)
long, deep hollow in ground made by a stream (6)
long, narrow shoal extending from the shore (8)
meet; hold a discussion (6)
miserable (7)
more self important (6)
narrow openings (8)
opponent (5)
outlawed (7)
plant with stiff pointy leaves (5)
plants armed stinging hairs (7)
remnants of a shipwreck (8)
ring-shaped ornament (7)
round leafy projection (4)
rounded hill of sand formed by the wind (4)
rubbing (7)
salty (8)
shocked;dazed (7)
sign; indication (4)
silly (5)
steep-sided high flatland (4)
tendons (6)
thin, cooked cereal (5)
think about (6)
thrashing (8)
trespassers (9)
twisted (9)
uproar (6)
winner (6)
with disapproval (13)

Blue Dolphins Vocabulary Word Search 3

ABALONES	FLAILING	MESA	SINEWS
CARCASS	FORBADE	NETTLES	SINGED
CHAFING	FORLORN	OMEN	STUNNED
CIRCLET	GALLEONS	PARLEY	STUNTED
CLAMOR	GIDDY	PERISH	TRINKETS
CORMORANTS	GNAWED	PITCH	VAINER
CREVICES	GRUEL	PONDER	VANQUISHED
CURATOR	HEADLAND	PROW	VICTOR
DECREED	INTRUDERS	PURSUER	WARILY
DETERMINATION	KELP	RAVINE	WARY
DUNE	LAIR	RESTRAIN	WRECKAGE
ENTANGLED	LEAGUES	RIVAL	YUCCA
EXCAVATIONS	LOBE	SANDSPIT	
FAGGOT	LURE	SHIRKERS	

Blue Dolphins Vocabulary Word Search 3 Answer Key

ABALONES	FLAILING	MESA	SINEWS
CARCASS	FORBADE	NETTLES	SINGED
CHAFING	FORLORN	OMEN	STUNNED
CIRCLET	GALLEONS	PARLEY	STUNTED
CLAMOR	GIDDY	PERISH	TRINKETS
CORMORANTS	GNAWED	PITCH	VAINER
CREVICES	GRUEL	PONDER	VANQUISHED
CURATOR	HEADLAND	PROW	VICTOR
DECREED	INTRUDERS	PURSUER	WARILY
DETERMINATION	KELP	RAVINE	WARY
DUNE	LAIR	RESTRAIN	WRECKAGE
ENTANGLED	LEAGUES	RIVAL	YUCCA
EXCAVATIONS	LOBE	SANDSPIT	
FAGGOT	LURE	SHIRKERS	

Blue Dolphins Vocabulary Word Search 4

```
T B P Z F G S Q C X P Y K H X Q L R N N
R R A M A F I P L Y J O S E B D C O T L
I A R Q G S N C Z M J X N A P P B M V R
N C L R G T G O B G S S D K I C A M R N
K K E F O F E B D R E J W L E L T L G T
E I Y N T S D R R U M S S A C R A C H W
T S O L L E B U G L D O S N R T I H P
S H M V W P A N J V E R D S I N H R V
Z M E A K O E N T E M H L A I A L O Y P
N S N O E L L A G A D S C D N R W E X P
X G E F L A J C C R E I I E E T Y X W
X S T G P B P C R C U R R T W S S W C Z
W H T S W A U U I T X E C S E S R V J
Q I L F T Y H V R S J P L R V R G A B
L R E R W U E G T S K F E M T R N C T F
W K S N K R N F Z B U L T I V I I K I L
M E F Z C D K T O F S E W N V J L A O D
T R O L O B E C E R U L R A I W I G N Q
J S R G C S B C E D L G R T C X A E S J
F G B H U W T D R F R O K I T Y L Z R Y
K I A J R A U U K E L Z R O O R F Y M S
W D D R A R P W N C E P V N R I V A L Y
Q D E L T Y X I C N P D C H A F I N G L
K Y X N O B A F G D E L G N A T N E J V
S R I K R V C T I P S D N A S Z S M C L
```

ABALONES	FAGGOT	LURE	SHIRKERS
BRACKISH	FLAILING	MESA	SINEWS
CARCASS	FORBADE	NETTLES	SINGED
CHAFING	FORLORN	OMEN	STUNNED
CIRCLET	GALLEONS	PARLEY	STUNTED
CLAMOR	GIDDY	PERISH	TRINKETS
CORMORANTS	GNAWED	PITCH	VAINER
CREVICES	GRUEL	PONDER	VICTOR
CURATOR	HEADLAND	PROW	WARILY
DECREED	INTRUDERS	PURSUER	WARY
DETERMINATION	KELP	RAVINE	WRECKAGE
DUNE	LAIR	RESTRAIN	YUCCA
ENTANGLED	LEAGUES	RIVAL	
EXCAVATIONS	LOBE	SANDSPIT	

Blue Dolphins Vocabulary Word Search 4 Answer Key

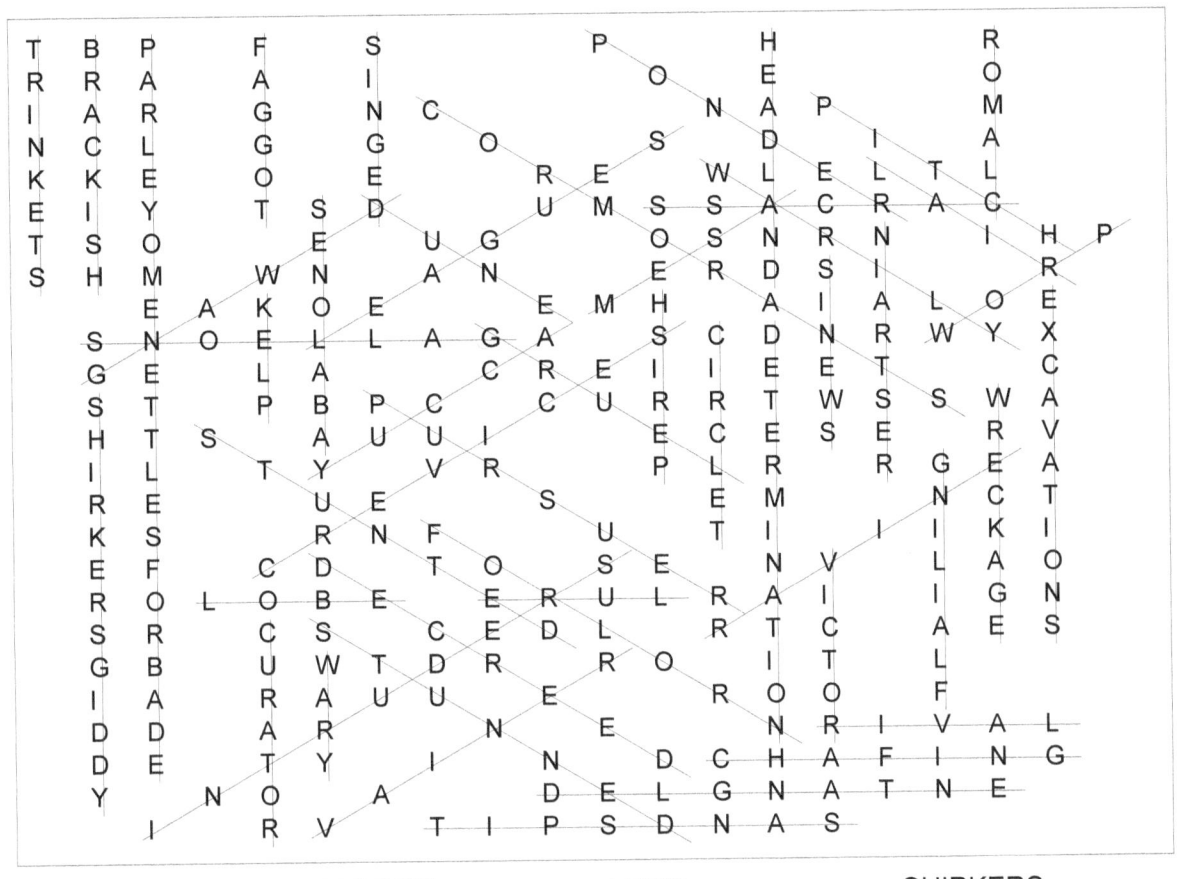

ABALONES	FAGGOT	LURE	SHIRKERS
BRACKISH	FLAILING	MESA	SINEWS
CARCASS	FORBADE	NETTLES	SINGED
CHAFING	FORLORN	OMEN	STUNNED
CIRCLET	GALLEONS	PARLEY	STUNTED
CLAMOR	GIDDY	PERISH	TRINKETS
CORMORANTS	GNAWED	PITCH	VAINER
CREVICES	GRUEL	PONDER	VICTOR
CURATOR	HEADLAND	PROW	WARILY
DECREED	INTRUDERS	PURSUER	WARY
DETERMINATION	KELP	RAVINE	WRECKAGE
DUNE	LAIR	RESTRAIN	YUCCA
ENTANGLED	LEAGUES	RIVAL	
EXCAVATIONS	LOBE	SANDSPIT	

Island Of The Blue Dolphins Vocabulary Crossword 1

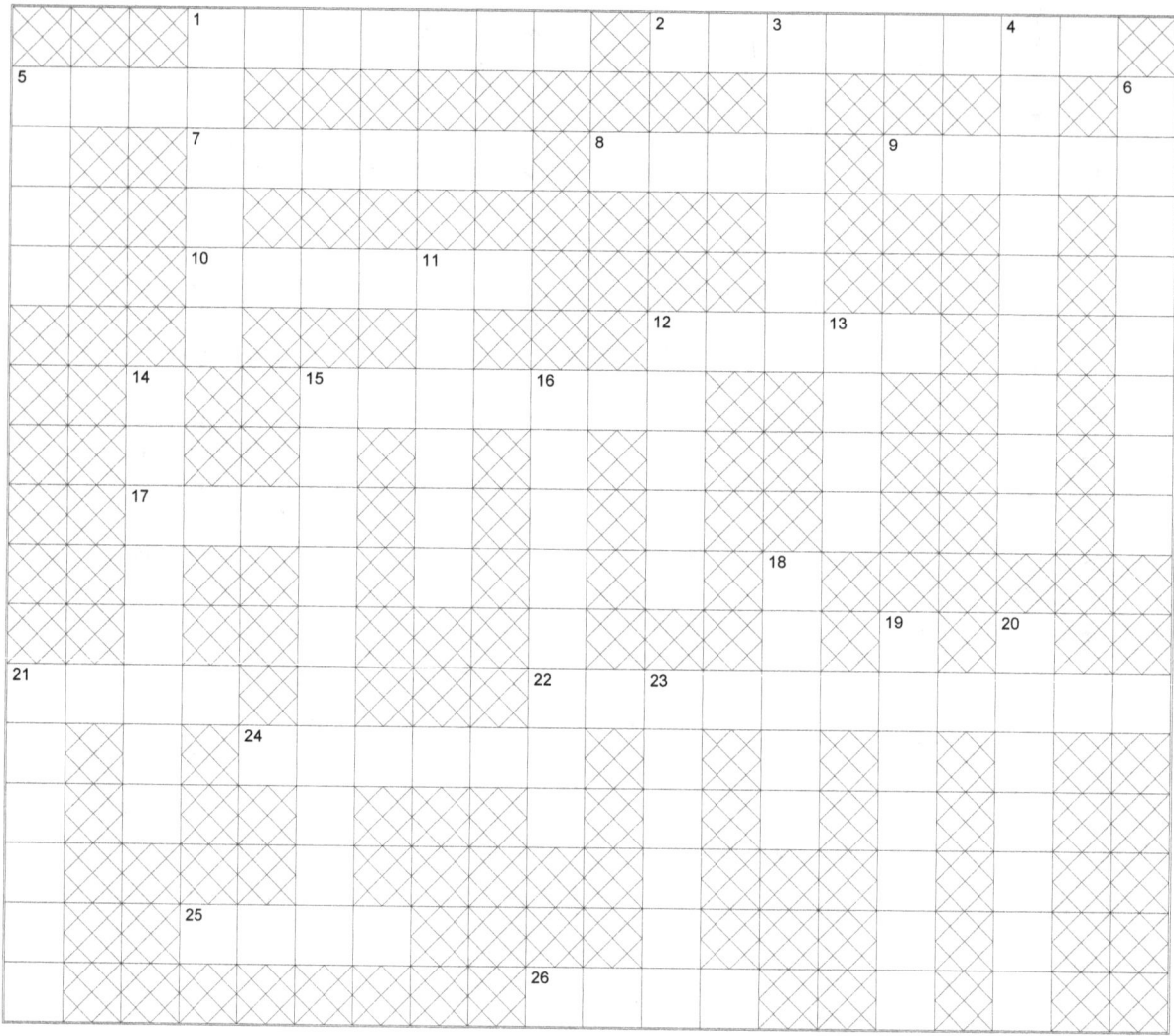

Across
1. hunter; tracker
2. hold back; control
5. round leafy projection
7. long, deep hollow in ground made by a stream
8. sign; indication
9. black, sticky tar or asphalt found along
10. tendons
12. silly
15. person in charge of a museum
17. den of wild animals
21. front end; bow
22. digs
24. bundle of sticks used for fuel
25. steep-sided high flatland
26. cautious

Down
1. die
3. burnt; scorched
4. trespassers
5. trap
6. loafers
11. cautiously
12. thin, cooked cereal
13. rounded hill of sand formed by the wind
14. large sailing vessels
15. large, web-footed sea birds
16. baubles; jewels
18. opponent
19. shocked; dazed
20. outlawed
21. meet; hold a discussion
23. uproar

Island Of The Blue Dolphins Vocabulary Crossword 1 Answer Key

			¹P	U	R	S	U	E	R		²R	³E	S	T	R	⁴A	I	N		
⁵L	O	B	E									I				N				⁶S
U			⁷R	A	V	I	N	E		⁸O	M	E	N		⁹P	I	T	C	H
R			I									G				R				I
E			¹⁰S	I	N	E	¹¹W	S				E				U				R
			H				A			¹²G	I	D	¹³D	Y		D				K
		¹⁴G			¹⁵C	U	R	A	T	¹⁶O	R		U			E				E
		A			O		I			R			N			R				R
		¹⁷L	A	I	R		L			I			E			S				S
		L			M		Y			E		¹⁸R							
		E			O		N			L		I				¹⁹S		²⁰F		
²¹P	R	O	W		R		K		²²E	X	C	²³A	V	A	T	I	O	N	S
A		N		²⁴F	A	G	G	O	T			L			A		U		R	
R		S		A					S			A			L		N		B	
L				N								M					N		A	
E			²⁵M	E	S	A						O					E		D	
Y				T				²⁶W	A	R	Y						D		E	

Across
1. hunter; tracker
2. hold back; control
5. round leafy projection
7. long, deep hollow in ground made by a stream
8. sign; indication
9. black, sticky tar or asphalt found along
10. tendons
12. silly
15. person in charge of a museum
17. den of wild animals
21. front end; bow
22. digs
24. bundle of sticks used for fuel
25. steep-sided high flatland
26. cautious

Down
1. die
3. burnt; scorched
4. trespassers
5. trap
6. loafers
11. cautiously
12. thin, cooked cereal
13. rounded hill of sand formed by the wind
14. large sailing vessels
15. large, web-footed sea birds
16. baubles; jewels
18. opponent
19. shocked; dazed
20. outlawed
21. meet; hold a discussion
23. uproar

Island Of The Blue Dolphins Vocabulary Crossword 2

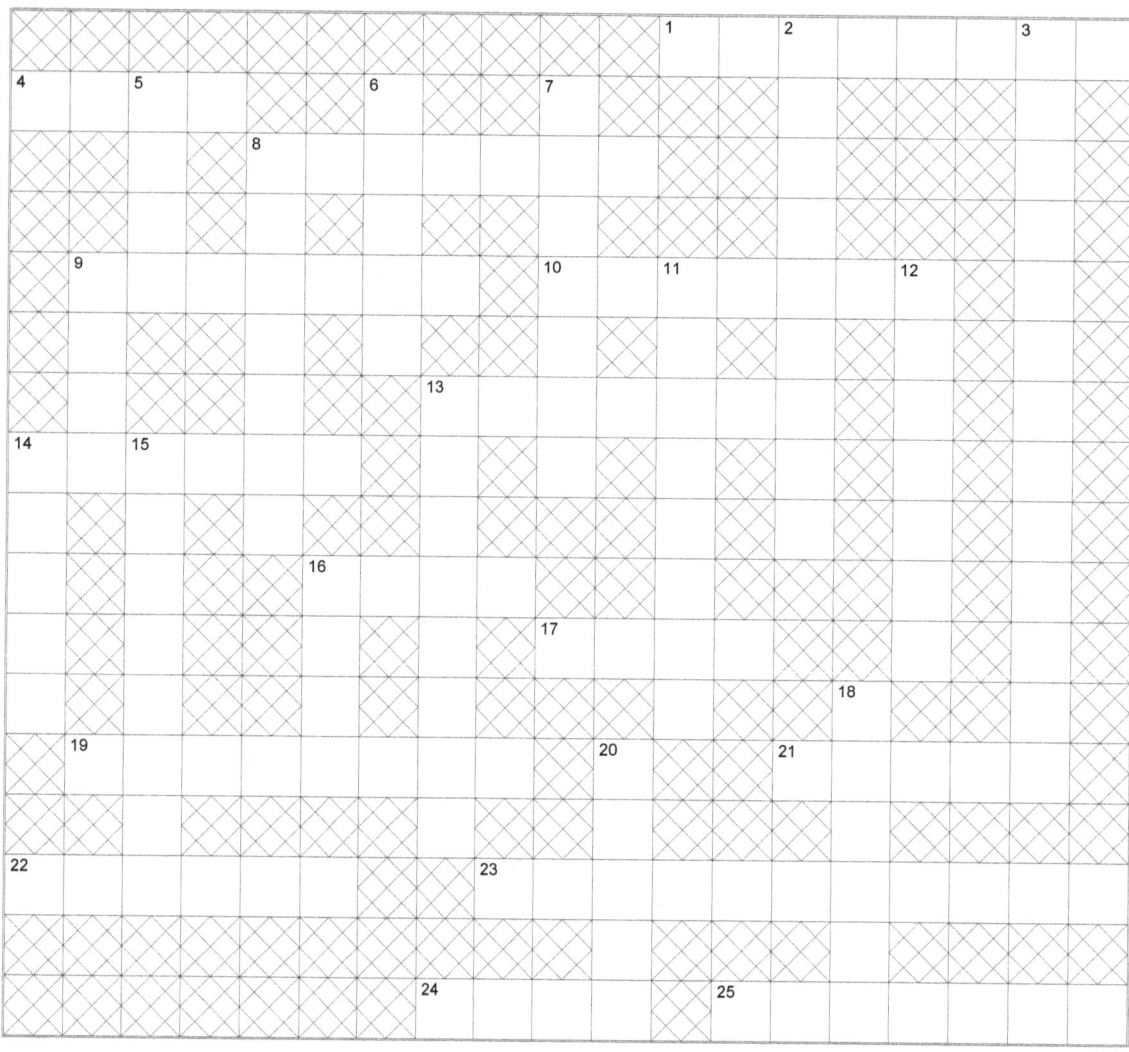

Across
1. loafers
4. coarse, brown seaweed
8. person in charge of a museum
9. ordered
10. three miles unit of measurement
13. outlawed
14. die
16. den of wild animals
17. sign; indication
19. large sailing vessels
21. silly
22. burnt;scorched
23. digs
24. steep-sided high flatland
25. ring-shaped ornament

Down
2. trespassers
3. with disapproval
5. trap
6. thin, cooked cereal
7. miserable
8. dead animal body
9. rounded hill of sand formed by the wind
11. edible shellfish
12. shocked;dazed
13. thrashing
14. black, sticky tar or asphalt found along
15. hold back; control
16. round leafy projection
18. winner
20. plant with stiff pointy leaves

Island Of The Blue Dolphins Vocabulary Crossword 2 Answer Key

											¹S	H	²I	R	K	E	³R	S
⁴K	E	⁵L	P			⁶G		⁷F					N				E	
		U		⁸C	U	R	A	T	O	R			T				P	
		R		A		U		R					R				R	
		⁹D	E	C	R	E	E	D		¹⁰L	¹¹E	A	G	U	E	¹²S		O
		U		C		L		O			B		D			T		A
		N		A		¹³F	O	R	B	A	D	E				U		C
¹⁴P	E	¹⁵R	I	S	H		L		N		L		R			N		H
I		E		S			A				O		S			N		F
T		S		¹⁶L	A	I	R				N					E		U
C		T		O			L		¹⁷O	M	E	N			¹⁸D		L
H		R		B			I		S					V			L
	¹⁹G	A	L	L	E	O	N	S		²⁰Y		²¹G	I	D	D	Y
		I				G				U		C				
²²S	I	N	G	E	D		²³E	X	C	A	V	A	T	I	O	N	S
									C			O				
						²⁴M	E	S	A		²⁵C	I	R	C	L	E	T

Across
1. loafers
4. coarse, brown seaweed
8. person in charge of a museum
9. ordered
10. three miles unit of measurement
13. outlawed
14. die
16. den of wild animals
17. sign; indication
19. large sailing vessels
21. silly
22. burnt;scorched
23. digs
24. steep-sided high flatland
25. ring-shaped ornament

Down
2. trespassers
3. with disapproval
5. trap
6. thin, cooked cereal
7. miserable
8. dead animal body
9. rounded hill of sand formed by the wind
11. edible shellfish
12. shocked;dazed
13. thrashing
14. black, sticky tar or asphalt found along
15. hold back; control
16. round leafy projection
18. winner
20. plant with stiff pointy leaves

Island Of The Blue Dolphins Vocabulary Crossword 3

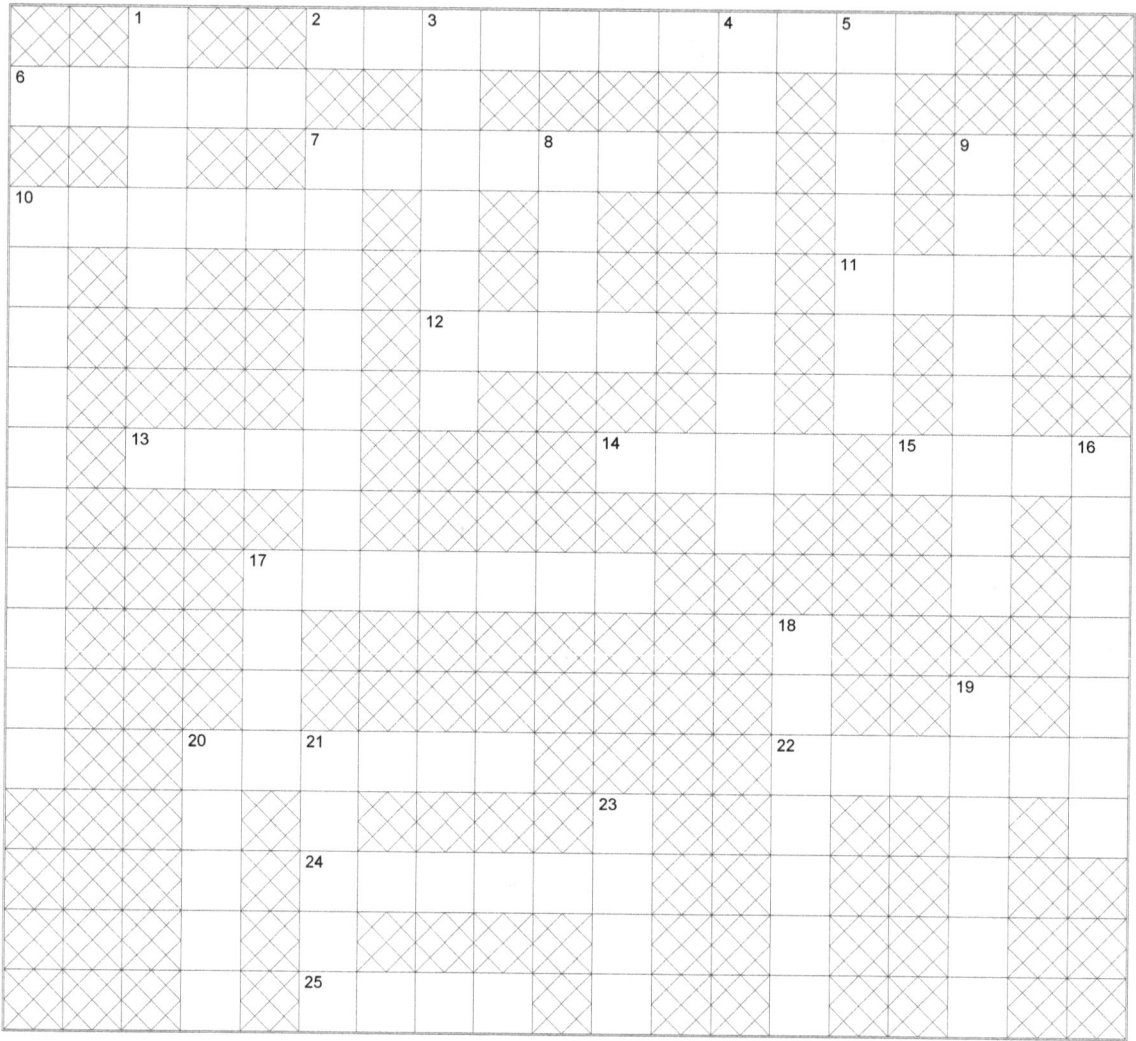

Across
2. digs
6. thin, cooked cereal
7. cautiously
10. winner
11. den of wild animals
12. sign; indication
13. steep-sided high flatland
14. cautious
15. coarse, brown seaweed
17. ordered
20. die
22. long, deep hollow in ground made by a stream
24. more self important
25. round leafy projection

Down
1. plant with stiff pointy leaves
3. person in charge of a museum
4. trespassers
5. plants armed stinging hairs
7. wreckage
8. trap
9. loafers
10. defeated
16. hunter; tracker
17. rounded hill of sand formed by the wind
18. miserable
19. burnt; scorched
20. black, sticky tar or asphalt found along
21. opponent
23. front end; bow

Island Of The Blue Dolphins Vocabulary Crossword 3 Answer Key

	1 Y		2 E	X	3 C	A	4 V	A	T	5 I	O	N	S	
6 G	R	U	E	L		U				N		E		
		C		7 W	A	R	I	8 L	Y	T		T		9 S
10 V	I	C	T	O	R		A	U		R		T		H
A		A		E		T		R		U		11 L	A	I	R
N				C		12 O	M	E	N		D		E		R
Q				K		R					E		S		K
13 U		M	E	S	A			14 W	A	R	Y		15 K	E	L	16 P
I				G				S					R		U
S			17 D	E	C	R	E	E	D				S		R
H			U							18 F				S
E			N							O		19 S		U
D		20 P	E	21 R	I	S	H		22 R	A	V	I	N	E
		I		I				23 P		L		N		R
		24 T		V	A	I	N	E	R		O		G	
		C		A				R		R		E	
		H		25 L	O	B	E		W		N		D	

Across
- 2. digs
- 6. thin, cooked cereal
- 7. cautiously
- 10. winner
- 11. den of wild animals
- 12. sign; indication
- 13. steep-sided high flatland
- 14. cautious
- 15. coarse, brown seaweed
- 17. ordered
- 20. die
- 22. long, deep hollow in ground made by a stream
- 24. more self important
- 25. round leafy projection

Down
- 1. plant with stiff pointy leaves
- 3. person in charge of a museum
- 4. trespassers
- 5. plants armed stinging hairs
- 7. wreckage
- 8. trap
- 9. loafers
- 10. defeated
- 16. hunter; tracker
- 17. rounded hill of sand formed by the wind
- 18. miserable
- 19. burnt; scorched
- 20. black, sticky tar or asphalt found along
- 21. opponent
- 23. front end; bow

Island Of The Blue Dolphins Vocabulary Crossword 4

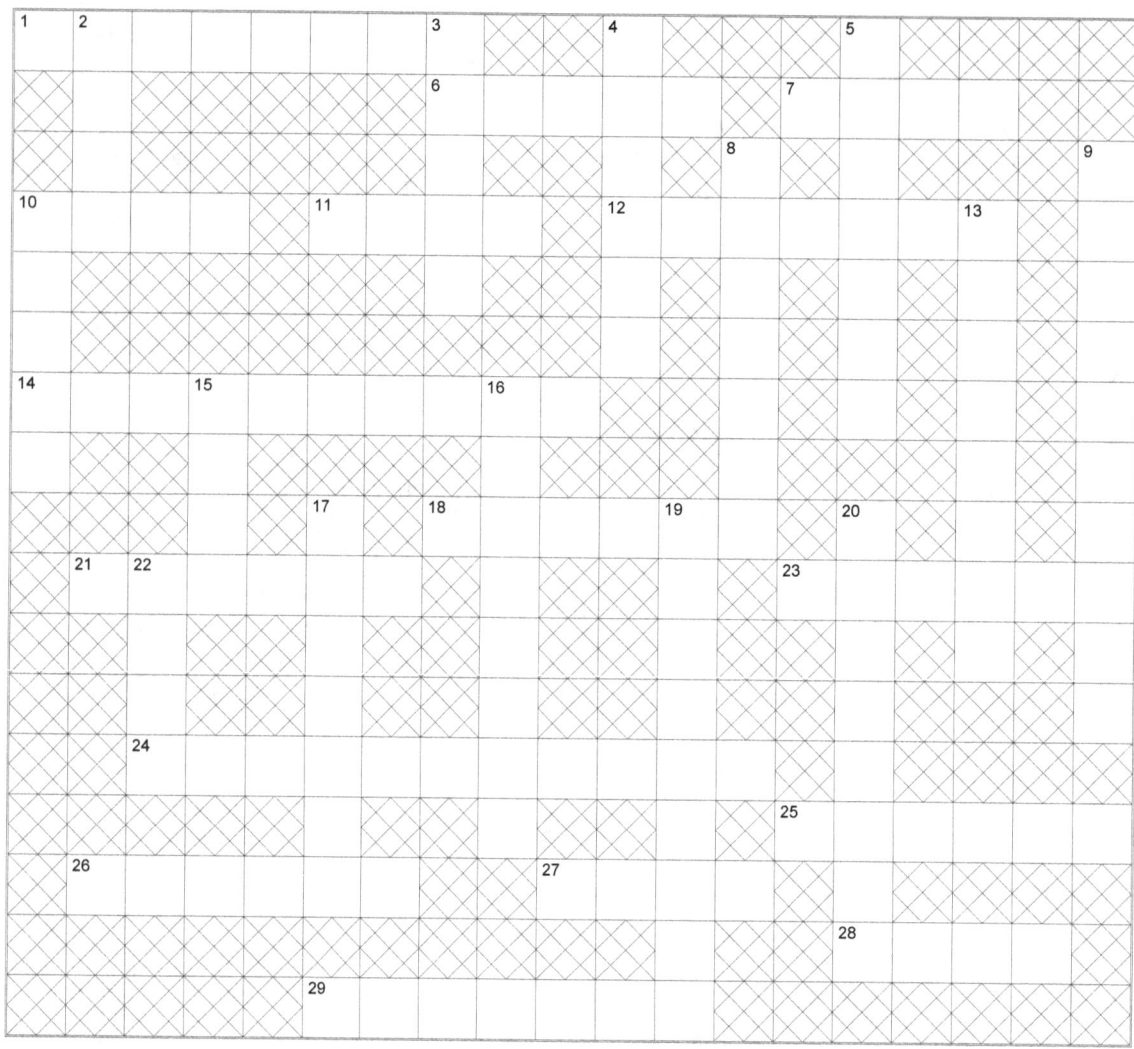

Across
1. thrashing
6. opponent
7. round leafy projection
10. front end; bow
11. sign; indication
12. plants armed stinging hairs
14. large, web-footed sea birds
18. burnt; scorched
21. uproar
23. die
24. digs
25. bundle of sticks used for fuel
26. chewed
27. coarse, brown seaweed
28. rounded hill of sand formed by the wind
29. ordered

Down
2. den of wild animals
3. thin, cooked cereal
4. more self important
5. miserable
8. shortened
9. defeated
10. black, sticky tar or asphalt found along
13. long, narrow shoal extending from the shore
15. steep-sided high flatland
16. baubles; jewels
17. outlawed
19. twisted
20. high point of land or rock extending into sea
22. trap

Island Of The Blue Dolphins Vocabulary Crossword 4 Answer Key

	1 F	2 L	A	I	L	I	N	G		4 V				5 F		
		A					6 R	I	V	A	L		7 L	O	B	E
		I					U			I		8 S		R			9 V
10 P	R	O	W		11 O	M	E	N		12 N	E	T	T	L	E	13 S	A
I					L					E		U		O		A	N
T										R		N		R		N	Q
14 C	O	15 R	M	O	R	A	16 N	T	S			T		N		D	U
H		E					R					E				S	I
		S		17 F		18 S	I	N	G	19 E	D	20 H		P			S
	21 C	22 L	A	M	O	R		N		N		23 P	E	R	I	S	H
		U		O		B		K		T		A		T			E
		R		R				E		A		D					D
		24 E	X	C	A	V	A	T	I	O	N	S		L			
		D				S				N			25 F	A	G	G	O	T
	26 G	N	A	W	E	D		27 K	E	L	P		N			
									E				28 D	U	N	E
				29 D	E	C	R	E	E	D						

Across
1. thrashing
6. opponent
7. round leafy projection
10. front end; bow
11. sign; indication
12. plants armed stinging hairs
14. large, web-footed sea birds
18. burnt; scorched
21. uproar
23. die
24. digs
25. bundle of sticks used for fuel
26. chewed
27. coarse, brown seaweed
28. rounded hill of sand formed by the wind
29. ordered

Down
2. den of wild animals
3. thin, cooked cereal
4. more self important
5. miserable
8. shortened
9. defeated
10. black, sticky tar or asphalt found along
13. long, narrow shoal extending from the shore
15. steep-sided high flatland
16. baubles; jewels
17. outlawed
19. twisted
20. high point of land or rock extending into sea
22. trap

Blue Dolphins Vocabulary Juggle Letters 1

1. RSAACSC = 1. _____
   dead animal body

2. SNUHEQAIDV = 2. _____
   defeated

3. RSEHPI = 3. _____
   die

4. OEBL = 4. _____
   round leafy projection

5. WENDAG = 5. _____
   chewed

6. DYGDI = 6. _____
   silly

7. EUURSRP = 7. _____
   hunter; tracker

8. LPEK = 8. _____
   coarse, brown seaweed

9. RSDERUITN = 9. _____
   trespassers

10. ACRROSTONM =10. _____
    large, web-footed sea birds

11. ICSHRBAK =11. _____
    salty

12. DAENLDHA =12. _____
    high point of land or rock extending into sea

13. LRIAV =13. _____
    opponent

14. DINGSE =14. _____
    burnt;scorched

15. DTEUSNT =15. _____
    shortened

Blue Dolphins Vocabulary Juggle Letters 1 Answer Key

1. RSAACSC = 1. CARCASS
   dead animal body

2. SNUHEQAIDV = 2. VANQUISHED
   defeated

3. RSEHPI = 3. PERISH
   die

4. OEBL = 4. LOBE
   round leafy projection

5. WENDAG = 5. GNAWED
   chewed

6. DYGDI = 6. GIDDY
   silly

7. EUURSRP = 7. PURSUER
   hunter; tracker

8. LPEK = 8. KELP
   coarse, brown seaweed

9. RSDERUITN = 9. INTRUDERS
   trespassers

10. ACRROSTONM = 10. CORMORANTS
    large, web-footed sea birds

11. ICSHRBAK = 11. BRACKISH
    salty

12. DAENLDHA = 12. HEADLAND
    high point of land or rock extending into sea

13. LRIAV = 13. RIVAL
    opponent

14. DINGSE = 14. SINGED
    burnt; scorched

15. DTEUSNT = 15. STUNTED
    shortened

Blue Dolphins Vocabulary Juggle Letters 2

1. NMOE = 1. _____
   sign; indication

2. NLFRORO = 2. _____
   miserable

3. UDNSENT = 3. _____
   shocked; dazed

4. BOLE = 4. _____
   round leafy projection

5. EMAS = 5. _____
   steep-sided high flatland

6. ANLSGOLE = 6. _____
   large sailing vessels

7. RCALMO = 7. _____
   uproar

8. VRINAE = 8. _____
   long, deep hollow in ground made by a stream

9. TAFOGG = 9. _____
   bundle of sticks used for fuel

10. OEAEITTNRNDIM = 10. _____
    conviction

11. LETTNES = 11. _____
    plants armed stinging hairs

12. ALIR = 12. _____
    den of wild animals

13. UYCCA = 13. _____
    plant with stiff pointy leaves

14. IAWRYL = 14. _____
    cautiously

15. AEHNDADL = 15. _____
    high point of land or rock extending into sea

Blue Dolphins Vocabulary Juggle Letters 2 Answer Key

1. NMOE = 1. OMEN
   sign; indication

2. NLFRORO = 2. FORLORN
   miserable

3. UDNSENT = 3. STUNNED
   shocked; dazed

4. BOLE = 4. LOBE
   round leafy projection

5. EMAS = 5. MESA
   steep-sided high flatland

6. ANLSGOLE = 6. GALLEONS
   large sailing vessels

7. RCALMO = 7. CLAMOR
   uproar

8. VRINAE = 8. RAVINE
   long, deep hollow in ground made by a stream

9. TAFOGG = 9. FAGGOT
   bundle of sticks used for fuel

10. OEAEITTNRNDIM = 10. DETERMINATION
    conviction

11. LETTNES = 11. NETTLES
    plants armed stinging hairs

12. ALIR = 12. LAIR
    den of wild animals

13. UYCCA = 13. YUCCA
    plant with stiff pointy leaves

14. IAWRYL = 14. WARILY
    cautiously

15. AEHNDADL = 15. HEADLAND
    high point of land or rock extending into sea

Copyrighted

Blue Dolphins Vocabulary Juggle Letters 3

1. NUDTETS = 1. _____
   shortened

2. ERDECDE = 2. _____
   ordered

3. LEETNST = 3. _____
   plants armed stinging hairs

4. KNIRTTES = 4. _____
   baubles; jewels

5. ESMA = 5. _____
   steep-sided high flatland

6. IREHPS = 6. _____
   die

7. TCHIP = 7. _____
   black, sticky tar or asphalt found along

8. ICCVREES = 8. _____
   narrow openings

9. EAVINR = 9. _____
   more self important

10. ARSACCS =10. _____
    dead animal body

11. MIIENTERONDAT =11. _____
    conviction

12. OMOCSTNRRA =12. _____
    large, web-footed sea birds

13. ENUD =13. _____
    rounded hill of sand formed by the wind

14. AKCEWEGR =14. _____
    remnants of a shipwreck

15. DWGNAE =15. _____
    chewed

Blue Dolphins Vocabulary Juggle Letters 3 Answer Key

1. NUDTETS = 1. STUNTED
shortened

2. ERDECDE = 2. DECREED
ordered

3. LEETNST = 3. NETTLES
plants armed stinging hairs

4. KNIRTTES = 4. TRINKETS
baubles; jewels

5. ESMA = 5. MESA
steep-sided high flatland

6. IREHPS = 6. PERISH
die

7. TCHIP = 7. PITCH
black, sticky tar or asphalt found along

8. ICCVREES = 8. CREVICES
narrow openings

9. EAVINR = 9. VAINER
more self important

10. ARSACCS = 10. CARCASS
dead animal body

11. MIIENTERONDAT = 11. DETERMINATION
conviction

12. OMOCSTNRRA = 12. CORMORANTS
large, web-footed sea birds

13. ENUD = 13. DUNE
rounded hill of sand formed by the wind

14. AKCEWEGR = 14. WRECKAGE
remnants of a shipwreck

15. DWGNAE = 15. GNAWED
chewed

Copyrighted

Blue Dolphins Vocabulary Juggle Letters 4

1. TENEITRONIDAM = 1. _____
   conviction

2. GATOFG = 2. _____
   bundle of sticks used for fuel

3. TRDRISNUE = 3. _____
   trespassers

4. DDYGI = 4. _____
   silly

5. AGHCFNI = 5. _____
   rubbing

6. LVIAR = 6. _____
   opponent

7. MALRCO = 7. _____
   uproar

8. ALRI = 8. _____
   den of wild animals

9. RBFAEOD = 9. _____
   outlawed

10. NLEALGOS = 10. _____
    large sailing vessels

11. OALNSEBA = 11. _____
    edible shellfish

12. OAXACTNVSIE = 12. _____
    digs

13. ERVINA = 13. _____
    long, deep hollow in ground made by a stream

14. IRRSHEKS = 14. _____
    loafers

15. SWINSE = 15. _____
    tendons

Blue Dolphins Vocabulary Juggle Letters 4 Answer Key

1. TENEITRONIDAM = 1. DETERMINATION
conviction

2. GATOFG = 2. FAGGOT
bundle of sticks used for fuel

3. TRDRISNUE = 3. INTRUDERS
trespassers

4. DDYGI = 4. GIDDY
silly

5. AGHCFNI = 5. CHAFING
rubbing

6. LVIAR = 6. RIVAL
opponent

7. MALRCO = 7. CLAMOR
uproar

8. ALRI = 8. LAIR
den of wild animals

9. RBFAEOD = 9. FORBADE
outlawed

10. NLEALGOS = 10. GALLEONS
large sailing vessels

11. OALNSEBA = 11. ABALONES
edible shellfish

12. OAXACTNVSIE = 12. EXCAVATIONS
digs

13. ERVINA = 13. RAVINE
long, deep hollow in ground made by a stream

14. IRRSHEKS = 14. SHIRKERS
loafers

15. SWINSE = 15. SINEWS
tendons

ABALONES	edible shellfish
BRACKISH	salty
CARCASS	dead animal body
CHAFING	rubbing
CIRCLET	ring-shaped ornament
CLAMOR	uproar

CORMORANTS	large, web-footed sea birds
CREVICES	narrow openings
CURATOR	person in charge of a museum
DECREED	ordered
DETERMINATION	conviction
DUNE	rounded hill of sand formed by the wind

ENTANGLED	twisted
EXCAVATIONS	digs
FAGGOT	bundle of sticks used for fuel
FLAILING	thrashing
FORBADE	outlawed
FORLORN	miserable

GALLEONS	large sailing vessels
GIDDY	silly
GNAWED	chewed
GRUEL	thin, cooked cereal
HEADLAND	high point of land or rock extending into sea
INTRUDERS	trespassers

KELP	coarse, brown seaweed
LAIR	den of wild animals
LEAGUES	three miles unit of measurement
LOBE	round leafy projection
LURE	bait
MESA	steep-sided high flatland

NETTLES	plants armed stinging hairs
OMEN	sign; indication
PARLEY	meet; hold a discussion
PERISH	die
PITCH	black, sticky tar or asphalt found along
PONDER	think about

PROW	front end; bow
PURSUER	hunter; tracker
RAVINE	long, deep hollow in ground made by a stream
REPROACHFULLY	with disapproval
RESTRAIN	hold back; control
RIVAL	opponent

SANDSPIT	long, narrow shoal extending from the shore
SHIRKERS	loafers
SINEWS	tendons
SINGED	burnt; scorched
STUNNED	shocked; dazed
STUNTED	shortened

TRINKETS	baubles; jewels
VAINER	more self important
VANQUISHED	defeated
VICTOR	winner
WARILY	cautiously
WARY	cautious

WRECKAGE	remnants of a shipwreck
YUCCA	plant with stiff pointy leaves

Blue Dolphins Vocabulary

INTRUDERS	PERISH	WRECKAGE	STUNTED	GNAWED
MESA	SANDSPIT	OMEN	SINGED	FAGGOT
VICTOR	GRUEL	FREE SPACE	GALLEONS	FORBADE
STUNNED	RAVINE	PARLEY	LOBE	TRINKETS
EXCAVATIONS	CHAFING	CORMORANTS	VANQUISHED	ABALONES

Blue Dolphins Vocabulary

RESTRAIN	YUCCA	VAINER	WARY	BRACKISH
CREVICES	WARILY	PROW	PITCH	LAIR
SHIRKERS	FORLORN	FREE SPACE	ENTANGLED	RIVAL
PURSUER	REPROACHFULLY	GIDDY	PONDER	KELP
DETERMINATION	DECREED	HEADLAND	CIRCLET	LURE

Blue Dolphins Vocabulary

GNAWED	CARCASS	PONDER	NETTLES	OMEN
LAIR	SINEWS	GALLEONS	YUCCA	DUNE
LURE	STUNTED	FREE SPACE	RESTRAIN	CURATOR
GRUEL	RIVAL	PERISH	DETERMINATION	MESA
GIDDY	VAINER	BRACKISH	VICTOR	ENTANGLED

Blue Dolphins Vocabulary

HEADLAND	CHAFING	SANDSPIT	CIRCLET	WARILY
FORLORN	LOBE	FORBADE	EXCAVATIONS	PARLEY
PURSUER	STUNNED	FREE SPACE	CORMORANTS	SINGED
REPROACHFULLY	KELP	TRINKETS	WARY	FAGGOT
WRECKAGE	CLAMOR	PROW	LEAGUES	PITCH

Blue Dolphins Vocabulary

GRUEL	YUCCA	PROW	OMEN	SINEWS
PARLEY	PONDER	SHIRKERS	PITCH	CHAFING
STUNTED	FORBADE	FREE SPACE	CLAMOR	MESA
LEAGUES	FLAILING	RAVINE	LOBE	WARILY
CARCASS	PERISH	PURSUER	VICTOR	RIVAL

Blue Dolphins Vocabulary

TRINKETS	STUNNED	WRECKAGE	GIDDY	FORLORN
SANDSPIT	HEADLAND	CORMORANTS	LAIR	REPROACHFULLY
GALLEONS	FAGGOT	FREE SPACE	RESTRAIN	BRACKISH
CURATOR	LURE	DUNE	ABALONES	EXCAVATIONS
CREVICES	NETTLES	WARY	SINGED	VAINER

Blue Dolphins Vocabulary

TRINKETS	FORLORN	CIRCLET	BRACKISH	KELP
LEAGUES	LAIR	CURATOR	CLAMOR	WARILY
CORMORANTS	EXCAVATIONS	FREE SPACE	SANDSPIT	YUCCA
CHAFING	WRECKAGE	REPROACHFULLY	SHIRKERS	OMEN
LURE	DETERMINATION	FORBADE	INTRUDERS	VAINER

Blue Dolphins Vocabulary

RESTRAIN	STUNTED	VICTOR	PURSUER	GRUEL
RIVAL	HEADLAND	SINEWS	GIDDY	FAGGOT
PARLEY	STUNNED	FREE SPACE	LOBE	DUNE
PONDER	NETTLES	FLAILING	ENTANGLED	WARY
GALLEONS	PITCH	RAVINE	GNAWED	CARCASS

Blue Dolphins Vocabulary

RESTRAIN	SANDSPIT	PERISH	CURATOR	MESA
ENTANGLED	GRUEL	FLAILING	WRECKAGE	CLAMOR
WARY	GIDDY	FREE SPACE	PARLEY	OMEN
HEADLAND	CREVICES	VICTOR	SINEWS	REPROACHFULLY
VAINER	FAGGOT	FORLORN	SHIRKERS	VANQUISHED

Blue Dolphins Vocabulary

GNAWED	RAVINE	SINGED	BRACKISH	LEAGUES
ABALONES	PITCH	FORBADE	DETERMINATION	EXCAVATIONS
STUNTED	LOBE	FREE SPACE	INTRUDERS	STUNNED
TRINKETS	LURE	DUNE	CORMORANTS	CIRCLET
WARILY	YUCCA	KELP	LAIR	PURSUER

Blue Dolphins Vocabulary

STUNNED	SANDSPIT	PITCH	DECREED	INTRUDERS
EXCAVATIONS	CREVICES	VAINER	CLAMOR	KELP
GRUEL	LAIR	FREE SPACE	VANQUISHED	GNAWED
DETERMINATION	CORMORANTS	GALLEONS	ENTANGLED	RIVAL
WARILY	RESTRAIN	SINGED	FORBADE	PURSUER

Blue Dolphins Vocabulary

DUNE	CARCASS	BRACKISH	SHIRKERS	PARLEY
WARY	SINEWS	WRECKAGE	RAVINE	FORLORN
NETTLES	LOBE	FREE SPACE	ABALONES	STUNTED
OMEN	LURE	VICTOR	FAGGOT	PONDER
TRINKETS	HEADLAND	FLAILING	LEAGUES	YUCCA

Blue Dolphins Vocabulary

CREVICES	FORBADE	MESA	RIVAL	LEAGUES
PERISH	VAINER	ENTANGLED	VICTOR	DECREED
EXCAVATIONS	STUNTED	FREE SPACE	SANDSPIT	GRUEL
STUNNED	BRACKISH	ABALONES	VANQUISHED	FLAILING
CURATOR	HEADLAND	PURSUER	PONDER	REPROACHFULLY

Blue Dolphins Vocabulary

GALLEONS	KELP	OMEN	SINEWS	RAVINE
PROW	DUNE	DETERMINATION	WRECKAGE	FORLORN
WARY	GNAWED	FREE SPACE	SHIRKERS	INTRUDERS
FAGGOT	RESTRAIN	GIDDY	NETTLES	WARILY
PITCH	CHAFING	CIRCLET	SINGED	PARLEY

Blue Dolphins Vocabulary

PROW	CHAFING	CREVICES	PERISH	SINEWS
KELP	FORBADE	TRINKETS	BRACKISH	LAIR
CURATOR	INTRUDERS	FREE SPACE	VICTOR	CARCASS
EXCAVATIONS	REPROACHFULLY	FORLORN	RIVAL	LURE
YUCCA	FLAILING	MESA	ENTANGLED	DETERMINATION

Blue Dolphins Vocabulary

CIRCLET	WARY	DUNE	RESTRAIN	DECREED
GRUEL	LEAGUES	PARLEY	WRECKAGE	FAGGOT
STUNNED	STUNTED	FREE SPACE	LOBE	NETTLES
VANQUISHED	PURSUER	VAINER	SANDSPIT	PITCH
SHIRKERS	WARILY	RAVINE	ABALONES	SINGED

Blue Dolphins Vocabulary

BRACKISH	MESA	RIVAL	YUCCA	NETTLES
WRECKAGE	SINGED	LEAGUES	GIDDY	DUNE
VAINER	SANDSPIT	FREE SPACE	CARCASS	GNAWED
STUNNED	WARILY	CIRCLET	LOBE	KELP
PONDER	VICTOR	HEADLAND	GALLEONS	FLAILING

Blue Dolphins Vocabulary

SINEWS	VANQUISHED	LAIR	GRUEL	ENTANGLED
PURSUER	STUNTED	ABALONES	OMEN	CLAMOR
RESTRAIN	DECREED	FREE SPACE	REPROACHFULLY	FAGGOT
EXCAVATIONS	DETERMINATION	WARY	CORMORANTS	PARLEY
TRINKETS	FORLORN	SHIRKERS	PITCH	CHAFING

Blue Dolphins Vocabulary

ENTANGLED	OMEN	FLAILING	CORMORANTS	VICTOR
GIDDY	CURATOR	LAIR	CREVICES	PARLEY
VAINER	DECREED	FREE SPACE	CLAMOR	EXCAVATIONS
PITCH	DUNE	GALLEONS	LURE	STUNTED
SANDSPIT	INTRUDERS	FAGGOT	FORLORN	TRINKETS

Blue Dolphins Vocabulary

GNAWED	KELP	STUNNED	SINGED	SHIRKERS
CIRCLET	HEADLAND	YUCCA	DETERMINATION	PURSUER
CARCASS	ABALONES	FREE SPACE	PERISH	BRACKISH
MESA	SINEWS	LOBE	PONDER	RIVAL
NETTLES	RESTRAIN	VANQUISHED	LEAGUES	WARY

Blue Dolphins Vocabulary

GNAWED	YUCCA	NETTLES	PURSUER	CHAFING
DUNE	REPROACHFULLY	GIDDY	KELP	SANDSPIT
ENTANGLED	PROW	FREE SPACE	WARY	CARCASS
INTRUDERS	OMEN	LAIR	WRECKAGE	FAGGOT
VANQUISHED	MESA	CURATOR	RESTRAIN	FLAILING

Blue Dolphins Vocabulary

LEAGUES	TRINKETS	STUNTED	LURE	FORBADE
PERISH	SINGED	CORMORANTS	PONDER	VICTOR
CLAMOR	BRACKISH	FREE SPACE	ABALONES	GALLEONS
PARLEY	RIVAL	CIRCLET	SINEWS	DECREED
VAINER	RAVINE	HEADLAND	GRUEL	LOBE

Blue Dolphins Vocabulary

PERISH	CARCASS	CURATOR	LAIR	FORLORN
PONDER	MESA	DECREED	VANQUISHED	SINGED
ENTANGLED	LURE	FREE SPACE	KELP	OMEN
INTRUDERS	VICTOR	CHAFING	FLAILING	WARY
LEAGUES	PURSUER	RIVAL	RESTRAIN	STUNTED

Blue Dolphins Vocabulary

HEADLAND	SANDSPIT	FAGGOT	SINEWS	WRECKAGE
CREVICES	PROW	STUNNED	RAVINE	REPROACHFULLY
BRACKISH	GALLEONS	FREE SPACE	CORMORANTS	GIDDY
DETERMINATION	NETTLES	LOBE	ABALONES	GNAWED
SHIRKERS	PARLEY	PITCH	TRINKETS	DUNE

Blue Dolphins Vocabulary

MESA	RIVAL	CORMORANTS	CREVICES	HEADLAND
STUNTED	SANDSPIT	FORBADE	GRUEL	GNAWED
YUCCA	PROW	FREE SPACE	ENTANGLED	CARCASS
WARILY	CIRCLET	GIDDY	EXCAVATIONS	PERISH
DETERMINATION	FAGGOT	SINGED	LEAGUES	ABALONES

Blue Dolphins Vocabulary

DECREED	VAINER	REPROACHFULLY	LURE	LAIR
RESTRAIN	NETTLES	INTRUDERS	BRACKISH	CLAMOR
WARY	PONDER	FREE SPACE	VICTOR	FORLORN
DUNE	PURSUER	GALLEONS	KELP	LOBE
SHIRKERS	TRINKETS	STUNNED	SINEWS	OMEN

Blue Dolphins Vocabulary

RESTRAIN	FORLORN	FAGGOT	STUNNED	SINEWS
SINGED	NETTLES	PURSUER	KELP	INTRUDERS
CLAMOR	PARLEY	FREE SPACE	FLAILING	CURATOR
STUNTED	DUNE	GNAWED	PROW	BRACKISH
CARCASS	RIVAL	MESA	VANQUISHED	OMEN

Blue Dolphins Vocabulary

GRUEL	PERISH	WRECKAGE	GIDDY	CIRCLET
VAINER	LURE	LOBE	DECREED	WARY
CHAFING	RAVINE	FREE SPACE	ABALONES	SANDSPIT
FORBADE	SHIRKERS	VICTOR	REPROACHFULLY	PONDER
LAIR	TRINKETS	CORMORANTS	HEADLAND	DETERMINATION

Blue Dolphins Vocabulary

CREVICES	PERISH	PITCH	FLAILING	MESA
RAVINE	SINGED	LEAGUES	WARY	FORLORN
ENTANGLED	GRUEL	FREE SPACE	DUNE	VANQUISHED
PROW	RESTRAIN	SANDSPIT	GNAWED	INTRUDERS
STUNTED	CHAFING	LURE	CIRCLET	BRACKISH

Blue Dolphins Vocabulary

NETTLES	PURSUER	LAIR	CORMORANTS	REPROACHFULLY
YUCCA	FORBADE	DETERMINATION	EXCAVATIONS	VAINER
WRECKAGE	HEADLAND	FREE SPACE	OMEN	STUNNED
GALLEONS	LOBE	ABALONES	PARLEY	SHIRKERS
DECREED	SINEWS	FAGGOT	TRINKETS	PONDER

Blue Dolphins Vocabulary

STUNNED	LURE	YUCCA	DETERMINATION	FLAILING
FAGGOT	REPROACHFULLY	KELP	GALLEONS	MESA
CURATOR	CIRCLET	FREE SPACE	BRACKISH	SINEWS
SANDSPIT	OMEN	PARLEY	CLAMOR	INTRUDERS
CORMORANTS	PURSUER	RAVINE	VAINER	WARILY

Blue Dolphins Vocabulary

HEADLAND	DUNE	VICTOR	PONDER	FORLORN
CARCASS	VANQUISHED	PROW	CHAFING	GRUEL
WRECKAGE	SHIRKERS	FREE SPACE	WARY	LAIR
NETTLES	LEAGUES	RESTRAIN	TRINKETS	DECREED
GIDDY	RIVAL	GNAWED	CREVICES	SINGED

www.ingramcontent.com/pod-product-compliance
Lightning Source LLC
Chambersburg PA
CBHW081454070526
44586CB00019B/2351